Here's the Story

Using Narrative to Promote Young Children's Language and Literacy Learning

Here's the Story

Using Narrative to Promote Young Children's Language and Literacy Learning

Edited by
Daniel R. Meier

Foreword by
María de la Luz Reyes

Teachers College, Columbia University
New York and London

Published by Teachers College Press, 1234 Amsterdam Avenue, New York, NY 10027

Grateful acknowledgment is made for permission to reprint the following:

Figure 10.1 from the book *Below* by Nina Crews. Copyright © 2006 by Nina Crews. Reprinted by permission of Henry Holt and Company, LLC.

Figure 11.1 from THE PAPER PRINCESS by Elisa Kleven, copyright © 1994 by Elisa Kleven. Used by permission of Dutton Children's Books, A Division of Penguin Young Readers Group, A Member of Penguin Group (USA) Inc., 345 Hudson Street, New York, NY 10014. All rights reserved.

Library of Congress Cataloging-in-Publication Data

Here's the story: using narrative to promote young children's language and literacy learning / edited by Daniel R. Meier.
    p.   cm.
    Includes bibliographical references and index.
    ISBN 978-0-8077-4979-1 (pbk.) —ISBN 978-0-8077-4980-7 (hardcover)
    1. Language arts (Early childhood) 2. Storytelling. 3. Children—Books and reading. I. Meier, Daniel R.
    LB1139.5.L35H47 2009
    372. 67'7—dc22   2008055107

ISBN 978-0-8077-4979-1 (paperback)
ISBN 978-0-8077-4980-7 (hardcover)

Printed on acid-free paper
Manufactured in the United States of America

16 15 14 13 12 11 10 09   8 7 6 5 4 3 2 1

*In memory of denise brown, a gifted teacher
and lover of stories for children and teachers . . .
may her gifts live on in the hearts and minds of the children she taught.*

Contents

Foreword

FROM TIME IMMEMORIAL stories have played a vital role in the lives of people around the globe—in every village, region, country, and continent. Stories emerge spontaneously as an integral part of conversations, in the retelling of events and in ordinary interactions with others. Oral stories have informed and entertained us, captivated our imagination, and linked us to our communal past as well as to our own diverse cultural histories.

The prominence of stories in young children's lives is indisputable. From infancy onward, children are soothed and comforted by lullabies, entertained by finger plays, rhymes, songs, and chants. Children's books contain a treasure trove of rich language with metaphors, rhythm, rhyme, cadence, predictability, and imagery that can smooth the progress of their early language and identity development and serve as a medium for socialization. Regardless of race, economic class, cultural background, or gender, narratives are a part of children's everyday lives, indeed, all our lives.

My little granddaughters are a constant reminder of the importance of story. "Nana, read to me," or "Nana, tell me a story" are occasions for strengthening familial bonds and nurturing a love of language and literacy. Generally, our story time ends with peals of laughter and a plea, "¡Otra vez!" or "Again, Nana!" and moves on to their own replaying of the story or recitation of their favorite phrases. A similar response to stories occurs everyday in homes, daycare centers, and classrooms, where caregivers and teachers use stories to capture children's attention and imagination. When they respond with "Again!" adults can be certain they have hooked children into essential literate practices that will form the foundation for further learning and, perhaps, a lifelong love of reading.

In our case, it is also an opportunity to promote language learning in English *and* Spanish, with the goal of advancing to biliteracy. I use stories with my granddaughters as a means to expanding their verbal expression, learning what interests them and what they understand of "the word and the world" (Freire & Macedo, 1987). I find myself retelling the same oral stories and finger plays my mother used to tell me when I was a child. In doing so I am cognizant of passing on cultural traditions to yet another generation and of connecting my granddaughters in an ephemeral but intimate way to my mother—a great-grandmother they will never meet. This is, indeed, the transformative *power of stories.*

In *Here's the Story,* Daniel Meier and the contributing authors in this volume focus on the role narratives can play to promote children's language and literacy. Each chapter offers the reader helpful, concrete examples of how they utilize stories as a springboard for learning. A unique feature of this book is that Meier brings together an ensemble of authors who not only understand child development as an academic subject, but who are themselves involved in working directly with young children on a daily basis. As a result, these authors present up-close and personal observations of how children both respond to and create their own stories in the process of learning. In addition, the book highlights the work and voices of two renowned children's book authors/illustrators, Nina Crews and Elisa Kleven, whose award-winning books have garnered great popularity among children and teachers. These authors provide a unique look into their creative processes and inner workings of writing books for children. Readers should find in these models valuable ideas for facilitating children's appreciation of stories.

In the era of No Child Left Behind (NCLB), with its scripted reading curricula and heavy emphasis on high-stakes testing, teachers find it difficult to create spaces for children "to proclaim themselves" through story (Dyson & Genishi, 1994). In this climate, *Here's the Story* shines like a bright light on a dark night. It underscores the fact that early childhood teachers' practice of using story as a tool for emergent language and literacy is the same tool that can be utilized effectively for more advanced literacy practices in later grades, because as human beings we will always have an innate need for story as we continue to discover and proclaim who we are through this medium. Readers will find this book helpful for thinking about the utility of narratives for a wide variety of instruction. Lastly, in an unintended way, perhaps, *Here's the Story* harkens teachers at all grade levels to rethink the role of story and re-inject it into their instruction as a way of infusing lifeblood into a current language arts curriculum that is hijacked by legislative mandates gone awry.

—*María de la Luz Reyes*
Professor Emerita, University of Colorado-Boulder

REFERENCES

Dyson, A., & Genishi, C. (Eds.). (1994). *The need for story: Cultural diversity in classroom and community.* Urbana, IL: National Council of Teachers of English.
Freire, P., & Macedo, D. (1987). *Literacy: The word and the world.* South Hadley, MA: Bergin and Garvey.

Acknowledgments

I thank the 14 contributors to this volume—Rebecca Akin, Erica Al-maguer, Nina Crews, Jeff Daitsman, Inas Deeb, Kim Hughes, Nadia Jaboneta, Valerie Jakar, Elisa Kleven, Lori Oldham, Patricia Sullivan, Todd Wanerman, Nathan Weber, and Gina Wilson. I especially thank Nina Crews and Elisa Kleven for allowing me to reprint their beautiful artwork in this book. I am honored to have worked with such a talented and eclectic group of contributors. Their experiences and talents and wonderful work with and for children are what make this book an unusual collection of dedicated voices for the power of story in children's language and literacy learning. I thank the contributors for believing in the project, trusting my judgment as a first-time editor, and for their timely submissions and careful editing and revising. I am indebted also to María de la Luz Reyes for writing her wonderful foreword.

I also thank Teachers College Press for continuing to publish my books. This marks my fifth book with the press, and I wish to thank Brian Ellerbeck, who first believed in my work and took my first book; Marie Ellen Larcada, for her wise suggestions on this edited volume, and her continued support of my work and writing; and Lori Tate and the Teachers College Press production staff for their care and attention to this volume.

I also knew from the beginning that I wanted to dedicate this book to the memory of denise brown, a friend and colleague who passed far too early for all of us who knew her. When she spoke to my graduate school classes, she always included my books in her book display, and I look forward to using this edited volume and carrying on a bit of her teaching spirit.

The memory, too, of my father's dedication and perseverance in writing books, something that he cannot do anymore, kept me believing in this book and pushing me forward as the editor of the volume. My father always believed in the power of the written word for giving voice to original work and intellectual ideas, and this is what I have tried to do with the 14 contributors in this volume.

Last, I thank Hazelle, Kaili, and Toby for giving me the time and support to put this book together. It is my hope that story retains a coveted spot in classrooms for Kaili and Toby and all children in our classrooms.

Here's the Story

Using Narrative to Promote Young Children's Language and Literacy Learning

Introduction

When people say to me, "What do you do?" I say, I tell stories from my
life." They say, "You must have a very interesting life." "No," I say, "But I tell
it well."

—Spalding Gray, The New Yorker (2007)

S TORIES ARE collections of spoken, gestured, drawn, and written words
that render and transform feelings, thoughts, imaginings, and experiences. Stories are critical for children's playful and powerful
language and literacy learning from birth through the elementary school
grades. But in our current climate of frequent testing and prescribed curriculum, stories are quickly losing their prominence as one of the hall-
marks of excellent language and literacy education. We must now reclaim
stories as a centerpiece for effective and creative teaching in the early
childhood and elementary school years. As Dinah Volk (personal communication, April 2007) notes,

> Stories reach back to the fundamentals of good teaching while looking
> forward to our complex world in which education must nurture children
> as critical actors and in which multiple cultures and languages are integral
> to everyday life. If we are concerned about effective language and literacy
> learning, then we must understand the power of children's narratives.

Children benefit from a deep and broad interweaving of stories in their
language and literacy learning—stories foster a lively interchange of ideas,
thoughts, and feelings for children about themselves, their worlds, and
each other. Stories speak to children's lives, interests, experiences, wishes,
and fears. And when told well, they have an inner and outer artistic beauty
that entices children into the world of language and literacy learning.

STORIES AND CHILDREN'S FIRST LANGUAGE LEARNING

Rich and engaging stories are full of sound and sense and meaning,
touching children's physical senses and promoting healthy first-language
development. When we engage with children in the routines of everyday

life, whether changing an infant's diaper or talking with an older child at dinner, we engage children with the dramatic unfolding of plot, meaning, character, setting, and other essential elements of stories. For Margaret Meek, Aidan Warlow, and Griselda Barton (1977), in "listening to stories or reading them, the child moves outwards from himself to the world of action, or inwards into his thoughts and feelings" (p. 9). Stories can provide children with an internal and external bridge between self and others, helping them see the power of spoken, written, drawn, and dramatized words to engage an audience and express meaning.

Stories are also akin to the rhythm and tenor of song and music. The poet Peter Money (2000) writes in his poem "What We Do": "Birds singing is a language/Birds sing all the time/Bird's language is singing?/Song is language elevated. . . ." (p. 31). Stories, a close cousin to song and music, are a form of "language elevated." And when stories gain a foothold in the life of educational settings—through telling and listening, art, dictation and drama, reading and writing—children gain valuable practice and experience with enriched and "elevated" language. They learn to predict, mimic, and reinterpret the movement, plot, voice, character, time, place, languages, ideas, and feelings of the world of stories.

Nancy Mellon (2000) writes that "imaginative stories are often rooted in patterns of the human soul only slightly bound to the material world" (p. 55). Stories can provide children with the language of the imagination and imagined worlds far away. As teachers, we are children's earliest and closest partners in making and telling stories, for children "need adults to connect words and objects; words and feelings; words and deeds" (p. 119). For first-language learning, young children primarily learn and grow through play and the language of play. As we show and engage children in playful language arts (listening, speaking, reading, writing), dramatic arts (drama), and creative arts (drawing, painting, sculpture), we foster a playful foundation for language learning based on discovery, creativity, and mastery.

Since play is the primary vehicle for young's children's learning, and sociodramatic play is a potentially powerful influence on children's language development, linking stories and play provides children with powerful tools for making discoveries, imagining new possibilities, and composing new ideas. In both play and stories, children feel a sense of power, control, and meaning in their lives. Vivian Paley (1981) notes:

> A child's story often refocuses an event as if to view it from the outside. Characters are disguised and placed in different settings. Something that is difficult to understand in one context may seem more real in another.

Whether the event is of lasting importance or merely of fleeting interest, the child seeks to dominate the experience by placing his own framework around it. (pp. 158–159)

Paley (1990) also believes that "play and its necessary core of storytelling are the primary realities . . . and they may well be the prototypes for imaginative endeavors throughout our lives" (p. 6). Stories and play extend children's creativity and imagination, and when story and play are combined with drama, children become more aware of the power of language. For Paley (1981), "in acting out a story, the child must be more conscious of language than he is in free play. . . . He can use his own words, but he must remain within the structure of the story" (p. 167).

STORIES AND CHILDREN'S MULTILINGUAL LEARNING

For children learning English and other languages as they also learn literacy, a helpful term comes from Eve Gregory (2008): "new language learners." These are "children who may be at an early stage of learning or simply lack fluency in the language they need to read and write" (p. 14). For new language learners, stories play a central role in promoting new language use and understanding both in terms of oral and written language development. For example, new language learners benefit from children's story books with appealing content, enticing visuals, interesting vocabulary, accessible syntactical or grammatical sentence structures, and varied and rich story formats and genres. English learners benefit from our role as teachers in modeling, guiding, and interpreting these story books in rich and engaging ways—explaining difficult and new vocabulary, acting out a complex story idea, relying on the visuals to illustrate the text, and much more. Excellent narrative-based strategies for new language learners include stories that promote academic language, stories written and told in multiple languages, stories that promote content transfer from a first to a second language, stories that bridge home and school languages, and stories that build on vocabulary understanding in more than language.

Stories come in many shapes and sizes and personalities, blowing across generations and cultures and traditions and languages. Intimately tied to family, community, worldview, language, and discourse, stories are close to children's hearts and sense of self. For new language learners, effective language and literacy instruction also must speak to children's inner experiences with stories. As the poet Jimmy Santiago Baca (1986) writes in his poem "Black Mesa," "I have a vision of mountain range/proportions/to speak the heart's language/To write the story of my soul . . . ." Stories reveal and share our lives and our inner souls as individuals and as members of particular communities and cultural traditions. So for new language learners, they need to tell and experience stories that reflect their innermost wishes, hopes, fears, and dreams.

Successful multilingual and multiliterate learning occurs when children feel and know that their Englishes, languages, identities, and traditions are honored, celebrated, and integrated into the fabric of classroom life and instruction. For Donald Macedo (1997), "it is through their own language that linguistic minority students will be able to reconstruct their history and their culture" (p. 275). In this way, stories are intimate influences on the future of children's lives and hold a hallowed place in teaching and education. Geneva Smitherman (2007) notes that "W.E.B. Du Bois teaches us that education is not the same as training; education must be about us and the language that we use and understand. The goal of education is not to make a living, but to make a life" (p. 155). Stories, full of anticipation and plot and the forward pull of narrative, can pull all children forward as confident and competent readers, writers, and thinkers.

STORIES AND CHILDREN'S LITERACY DEVELOPMENT

Stories from birth through the elementary years come alive in literacy education when we bring in critical elements of first- and second-language learning as well as as conversation, dialogue, brainstorming, questioning. Anne Haas Dyson (2000) discusses the multivoicedness of orality and literacy:

> Writers do more than recruit ideas from that sea [of voices]—they swallow its very words. Indeed, for Bakhtin (1986, p. 2), most written genres have been formed by "absorb[ing] and digest[ing]" simpler, usually oral, genres such as dialogue. Thus, our written voices are quite literally linked to the oral voices of others. (p. 60)

As Hilary Minns (1997) also observes, "Young children who have opportunities to talk their way through books can respond to characters and events and find ways of linking the meaning of the story with meanings in their own lives, all at a high intellectual level" (p. 125). Here is where stories help children integrate language, literacy, and the development of the mind. It is this "high intellectual level," reached through daily engagement with captivating stories and books, that especially nudges children toward new feelings, new ideas, new discoveries.

There are three critical ways to consider and ensure a greater role for stories in children's language and literacy development. First, we want children to interpret and generate rich and engaging stories that foster an engaging relationship between life experiences and the experiences of literacy. For example, when children write stories with a certain level of sophistication in form and content, this higher level of narration helps them reflect and see their lives in novel ways. As James Britton (1983) points out, "precisely how a child sees the relationship between experienced events and narrated events we clearly do not know; yet it must surely be the case that narrative form perceived in stories begins to influence the interpretations he makes of what happens to him" (p. 5).

Second, we want children to experience stories and storymaking as a literary and aesthetic act. For example, when children write a story that imitates, draws upon, or extends literary devices and strategies used by another author, they are initiating themselves into the evolving pantheon of authors and writers. The process of making one's own written texts into something of beauty and power also gives children commanding control over the aesthetic form and feel of their work. As Michael Armstrong (2006) observes, "learning to compose a literary work is what learning to read and write amounts to" (p. 177).

Third, we want children to take a critical and thoughtful stance in the story world. For example, when children have the right mix of pedagogical guidance and support, they can "go up against" a published or told story as well as compose a story that is new in form and content. For this to happen, children need to feel that they have something to say—about other's stories (which involves reading) and their own (which involves writing) — and that there is a certain personal and persuasive power behind their words and thoughts and ideas. As Vasquez (2004) advocates, it is important for children to "deconstruct" book texts to provide "a space to explore the social construction of truth and reality" (p. 121).

STORIES, REFLECTION, AND EDUCATIONAL CHANGE

The effectiveness of our language and literacy teaching is ultimately based on our own understanding and valuing of story in our personal and professional lives. In part, we can do this by seeing our language and literacy teaching as an evolving story, with its own twists and turns of plot and setting and character. As Gian Pagnucci (2004) puts it, "Narrative is a way of life . . . a set of beliefs . . . an ideology" (p. 44). Through our stories—remembered ones from our childhood, current ones from our adulthood—we can improve our teaching of children and our understanding of ourselves as adult learners. Stories help us conceptualize and formulate our teaching philosophy and help us observe and reflect on the value of story for children's language and literacy learning. Carol Witherell and Nel Noddings (1991) note that

> Stories and narrative, whether personal or fictional, provide meaning and belonging in our lives. They attach us to others and to our own histories by providing a tapestry rich with threads of time, place, character, and even advice on what we might do with our lives. The story fabric offers us images, myths, and metaphors that are morally resonant and contribute both to our knowing and our being known. (p. 1)

When children generate their own stories—whether told or acted out or written—these stories "provide us with a view into children's worlds and are a powerful tool for learning about children and the knowledge and experiences they bring to school" (Volk, 2008, personal communication).

When we teach children well, we plan well and think well on our feet. When we do this, we ourselves are critical actors in the unfolding teaching=learning equation, and we are central to the direction of stories in children's language and literacy learning. Projects, units, activities, books, everything that constitutes our curriculum and what we do to teach children, can all be broken down into scenes, vignettes, characters, and plots. These moment-by-moment and day-to-day narratives form the larger stories of our teaching and our children's learning. Narrative is, as Barbara Hardy (1977) points out, "like lyric or dance, [and] is not to be regarded as an aesthetic invention used by artists to control, manipulate, and order experience, but as a primary act of mind transferred to art from life" (p. 12). If we see teaching as an art, and stories as a "primary act of mind," then stories guide us and make us at the same time—moving us along in our teaching, reaching back to where we've been, and moving us forward to where we want to be.

ABOUT THIS BOOK

The contributors to this edited book bring their special talents and experiences to bear on the challenge of expanding the conceptual and pedagogical place of story in children's language and literacy learning. In putting this volume together, I have deepened and broadened my own understanding and appreciation for the role of story in early childhood and the elementary school years thanks to the process of working with these authors. I put this book together as one small way to counter current curriculum and policy that devalues and demotes the role of story in language and literacy education. This book also came about because in my work with teachers, I wanted to recommend a book that honors story and deepens our understanding of its value, but I could not find just the right kind of book.

So I asked several current and former students—Erica Almaguer, Gena Wilson, Todd Wanerman, Patricia Sullivan, Nadia Jaboneta, Nathan Weber, Lori Oldham, Kim Hughes—from the M.A. Program in Early Childhood Education at San Francisco State University where I teach. I asked these teachers to contribute to this volume because I know first-hand their commitment to children and families, and their talent and ability to stay close to children's linguistic and literate lives. I know that readers will benefit from hearing from these talented teachers and caregivers, and relating to their challenges, joys, and insights involving story and children's language and literacy learning. Taken together, the seven chapters written by these authors provide us with insights on story for children from birth to age 6.

I met Rebecca Akin, another contributor, through the Teacher as Researcher SIG (Special Interest Group) of the American Educational Research Association. I then visited her first-grade classroom in the Oakland Unified School District, and after my visit, asked Rebecca if she were interested in writing a chapter on the place of story in a highly scripted language arts curriculum in the primary grades.

I met Jeff Daitsman at a recent National Association of Education for Young Children conference in Chicago, and was impressed with his iniative and interest in language and literacy teaching. Jeff subsequently emailed me and began sending me wonderful examples of his preschoolers' story dictation. He sent more and more examples until the collection grew large enough to form an entire chapter.

I also wanted to include the voices and perspectives of children's book authors in this volume since children's books are frequently used in classrooms but we know little about authors' views on the place of story. I am delighted to have the contributions of Elisa Kleven and Nina Crews, one author from the west coast and one from the east coast who do different kinds of children's books. I met Elisa Kleven through my friend Jacqueline Omania, who has invited Elisa into her third-grade classroom to talk about her books with Jacqueline's students. Elisa gladly agreed to an interview, and so over the course of a delicious lunch at a local Chinese restaurant, we met to talk about her views on story and the creative process behind her picture books.

Nina Crews's books are full of inventive photography and playful connections with contemporary childhood. I use her picture books in presentations to teachers and also in my language and literacy work with children. Teachers love her books and children quickly and endearingly connect to Nina's characters. Through phone conversations and emails, Nina shared her experiences growing up with two well-known children's book authors as parents, her perspectives on what makes for an artful story and picture book, and how she constructs her own stories and books.

On a trip to Israel, I had the good fortune to meet Valerie Jakar, who works with teachers in Israel and East Jerusalem. She drove me around to her schools where I met the Israeli, Israeli Arab, and Palestinian teachers with whom she works and also met and talked with the children. On one of my last days in Jerusalem, Valerie introduced me to her good friend and colleague, Inas Deeb, a teacher educator in East Jerusalem. When I returned home to California, I wanted to extend my interest in education in this region of the world, and so I asked Valerie and Inas if they would contribute a chapter to this volume. Their cowritten chapter is a testament to crosscultural dialogue and cooperation in the Middle East, and the power of educational professionals working across language and cultural boundaries.

The three major sections of the book cover the most fundamental and critical foundations for language and literacy growth: first-language development, multilingualism, and literacy development. Each section focuses on the forms and functions of story across the developmental span of young children up to the age of 10.

The chapters in Part I, "Stories and Children's First Language Learning," were written by two infant/toddler teachers (coauthors), a toddler/preschool teacher, a family childcare provider, and a preschool teacher. In Chapter 1, Erica Almaguer and Gena Wilson describe and explain how stories foster intimate social connections with language for infants and toddlers. Chapter 2's author Todd Wanerman discusses in his chapter how he links story drama with the play of his toddlers. Patricia Sullivan describes in Chapter 3 how her 3- and 4-year-old children are drawn to and understand superheroes in a project that fosters critical language and thinking. And in Chapter 4, Nadia Jaboneta discusses the value of a professional storyteller working with her preschool children.

The chapters in Part II, "Stories and Children's Multilingual Learning," were written by a family childcare provider, a preschool teacher, two teacher educators (coauthors), and an elementary school teacher. In Chapter 5, Kim Hughes discusses how she used social stories to promote language learning and multilingualism in her home childcare setting. Nathan Weber discusses in Chapter 6 the valuable lessons he learned using wordless picture books as a teacher of preschool-age English learners. Chapter 7 author Lori Oldham shows important connections between home and school language use for her Kindergarten bilingual students. In the last chapter of this part, Chapter 8, teacher educators and colleagues

Inas Deeb and Valerie Jakar provide an international example of the value of story by focusing on a language and literacy project with Israeli and Palestinian elementary school children.

The chapters in Part III, "Stories and Children's Literacy Development," were written by a preschool teacher, a teacher educator interviewing two children's book authors, and a first-grade teacher. In Chapter 9, Jeff Daitsman discusses important themes in the dictated stories of his preschool students, and also his own journey in learning how to carry out story dictation with young children. The children's book author Nina Crews is interviewed in Chapter 10, sharing her views on stories and story books with Daniel Meier, who discusses how Crews's books can promote effective story dictation for preschool-age children. In Chapter 11, the children's book author Elisa Kleven discusses with Daniel Meier her views on what makes a well-told story and how she creates her picture books for preschool and elementary-age children. In Chapter 12, elementary school teacher Rebecca Akin reflects on the challenges and rewards of finding a place for engaging stories in a prescribed literacy curriculum.

Finally, in the Epilogue, I close the book with a brief discussion on key concepts, themes, and strategies in the book, and I reflect on hopeful new directions for story in language and literacy education in early childhood and elementary school.

REFERENCES

Armstrong, M. (2006). *Children writing stories*. Berkshire, UK: Open University Press.

Baca, J. S. (1986). *Black mesa poems*. New York: New Directions.

Bakhtin, M. M. (1986). *Speech genres and other late essays*. Austin, TX: University of Texas Press.

Britton, J. (1983). Writing and the story world. In B. M. Kroll & G. Wells (Eds.), *Explorations in the development of writing* (pp. 3–30). London: John Wiley & Sons.

Dyson, A. H. (2000). Writing and the sea of voices: Oral language in, around, and about writing. In R. Indrisano & J.R. Squire (Eds.), *Perspectives on writing: Research, theory, and practice* (pp. 45–65). Mahweh, NJ: Erlbaum.

Gregory, E. (2008). *Learning to read in a new language: Making sense of words and worlds*. London: Sage.

Hardy, B. (1977). Narrative as a primary act of mind. In M. Meek, A. Warlow, & G. Barton, *The cool web: The pattern of children's reading*, (pp. 12–23). London: The Bodley Head.

Macedo, D. (1997). English only: The tongue-tying of America. In A. Darder, R. Torres, & H. Gutierrez (Eds.). *Latinos and education* (pp. 269–278). New York: Routledge.

Meek, M., Warlow, A., & Barton, G. (1977). *The cool web: The pattern of children's reading*. London: The Bodley Head.

Mellon, N. (2000). *Storytelling with children*. Stroud, UK: Hawthorn Press.

Minns, H. (1997). *Read it to me now*. Berkshire, UK: Open University Press.

Money, P. (2000). *Finding it: Selecting poems*. Santa Barbara, CA: Mille Gracie Press.

Pagnucci, G. (2004). *Living the narrative life: Stories as a tool for meaning making*. Portsmouth, NH: Heinemann.

Paley, V. P. (1981). *Wally's stories*. Cambridge, MA: Harvard University Press.

Paley, V. P. (1990). *The boy would be a helicopter: The uses of storytelling in the classroom*. Cambridge, MA: Harvard University Press.

Shades of gray. *The New Yorker*, March 5, 2007, p. 34.

Smitherman, G. (2007). Afterword. In H. S. Alim & J. Baugh (Eds.), *Talkin black talk: language, education, and social change* (pp. 153–155). New York: Teachers College Press.

Vasquez, V. M. (2004). *Negotiating critical literacies with young children*. Mahwah, NJ: Erlbuam.

Witherell, C., & Noddings, N. (Eds.). (1991). *Stories live tell: Narrative and dialogue in education*. New York: Teachers College Press.

PART I

STORIES
and
CHILDREN'S FIRST
LANGUAGE LEARNING

Chapter 1

From Zero to Three: The Value of Stories for Young Children's Language Learning

ERICA ALMAGUER AND GENA WILSON

Erica Almaguer is an infant/toddler teacher at San Francisco State University's Associated Students Inc. Early Childhood Education Center. She received her B.A. in Child and Adolescent Development and her M A in Early Childhood Education. She is a certified trainer for WestEd's Program for Infant/Toddler Care, has previously worked in a literacy program with children in low-performing schools, and is also interested in children's language development.

Gena Wilson is an infant/toddler teacher at the Associated Students Inc. Early Childhood Education Center at San Francisco State University. She is a certified trainer for WestEd's Program for Infant/Toddler Care, and has an M.A. in Early Childhood Education. Gena has been providing continuity of care for children ages 6 months to 3 years, and supporting very young children through relationship-based care.

S HARING STORIES with infants and toddlers is an intimate experience for both young children and adults. It is a bonding moment that facilitates the formation of a secure relationship for children with their caregivers. When children feel secure in their relationships, they become more open emotionally to engaging in learning from these interactions. They are also more able to make meaning from their experiences and experience personal relationships as a kind of unfolding story. In close personal relationships, language plays a key role as young children con-

13

nect relevant information and talk about their experiences. One of our roles as teachers of very young children is to offer extended opportunities for sharing stories to promote language development. Early exposure to language-rich story activities also establishes a model for conversation that includes turn-taking skills, comprehension, nonverbal communication, collaboration, and the scaffolding of ideas and feelings.

In this chapter, Erica first discusses how her story sharing with infants and toddlers contributes to their emerging receptive and expressive language. Gena then describes how her process of shared reading facilitates the development of her 3-year-olds' language and comprehension skills.

ERICA'S STORY

For infants and young toddlers, the value of story begins with the feelings that stories suggest, and the associations children make when told a story, whether it is in print or oral. These positive feelings are then transferred to a yearning for more stories, more language play, and more interaction around stories with adults and peers. The earliest forms of stories are those told while infants are still in the womb. Once infants are born, they hear more stories, in particular lullabies. Lullabies can be passed down from generation to generation, can have cultural influences, and can even be made up. However, all lullabies share a lulling and soothing melody. This melody often captures the attention of infants and creates a sense of intimacy, calmness, safety, and a bond between adults and children—all factors that promote feelings of comfort and support children's own expressive language.

Baa Baa Black Sheep—A Lulling Story

As an infant/toddler teacher I conduct home visits for new families prior to the children entering my care. The parents and/or caregivers and I discuss children's routines and more importantly their individual eating, napping, and play preferences so that I can provide consistency with the infant's home experiences. Two years ago, I began a new 3-year rotation with a group of 13 infants ranging in age from 4 months to 13 months. Mary was 8 months old at the time, and it was her very first experience away from her mother and father. As the days passed she expressed her likes and dislikes, and I began to identify how best to meet her needs while she was in my care. However, naptime was still challenging for us.

Mary could be very tired, but struggled with pushing me away while wanting me to hold her at the same time. Linda, Mary's mother, and I revisited this struggle day after day. I explained to Linda my process of holding Mary while giving her enough space to turn away from me if she wanted to and said that I sang lullabies to Mary to soothe her. Finally, 2 weeks later, Linda suggested that I sing "Baa Baa Black Sheep" to Mary. This song was not one that I sang to Mary, but I gave it a try. I began Mary's naptime routine and she began to cry, so I hummed "Baa Baa Black Sheep" as I held her in my arms. I continued to hum the song as I entered the room and positioned us in the rocking chair, and for the first time Mary's cry was softer, hardly even a cry and more like a whimper. I held her against my body as we swayed back and forth, and I softly began to sing the words to her. Mary began to sink into my body and calmness seemed to overcome her as she stared at me, a calmness we had not experienced before. Slowly she began to drift to sleep as I continued to sing her the song, and when the song ended, I simply hummed it but her eyes instantly opened. I quickly sang the song again and repeated it until she was deeply asleep. Mary had such a deep connection not only with the melody of "Baa Baa Black Sheep," but the words as well; her mother had been singing it to her since before Mary was born.

Mary is 2 years old now and still in my care. She continues to have a strong connection with that lullaby/story and asks me to sing it during group time. To expand on her interest I have introduced felt props and woolen balls, and show them in the order they appear in the song. I now see that this storytelling activity has three components that contribute to Mary's and the other children's early language learning:

1. The auditory component of listening to words that children may or may not yet understand
2. The visual component of seeing what my rendition of the sheep and the other characters look like
3. The sensory component of touching soft wool in its refined state

These techniques and objects capture and sustain the child's engagement with lullaby stories.

Is It a Dish? No, It's a Fish!—Rhymes and Stories

Rhymes and repetition in stories also capture infants' attention and expose them to varied forms of oral language. When I began my second year providing continuity of care, my group of older infants were 14–25 months old. They instantly fell in love with *What Is It?* (2000) by Amy Allen. The children would often bring me this book and sit on my lap as their way of asking me to read it to them. It didn't take very long for the children to realize that after I would ask, "Is it a dish?," I would say "No, it's a fish!" This book soon became interactive, as I paused after asking "Is it a key?" and the children smiled at me and said "No!" Then, as I turned the page, they looked at me with excitement, anticipating what would appear on the page. As their syntax expanded, the children began completing the sentence before I had the chance to turn the page.

The book also allowed the children to visualize the shapes and make connections between concepts in the book and other items or books in the classroom. For example, Rosy, one of the teacher assistants, read the book to a group of children, and when she asked, "Is it a dish?", the children responded in chorus, "No, it's a fish!" Alex, 20 months old at the time, jumped up and ran over to Freddie, our class fish and exclaimed "Fweddie, fish!" Not only had Alex connected the fish in the book with the fish in our classroom, but he used oral and nonverbal language to express this discovery.

Kaylani, another child in my classroom who was 19 months old at the time, was also very fond of this book. Every day after naptime it became part of her wake-up routine to find this book and ask me to read it to her. One day Kaylani was in the reading area with another popular rhyming book, *Twinkle, Twinkle Little Star* (1997) by Iza Trapani, and was "reading" it to herself. Every time she flipped the page she mumbled unidentifiable words and then ended with "No, a [s]tar!"

In both instances, Alex and Kaylani borrowed a story they enjoyed and had heard repeatedly to expand their vocabulary and syntax and make meaning by linking elements of the books with other aspects of classroom life.

He Was as Tall as a Tree, and Could Eat Sheep in One Gulp!

As the year progressed, I told individual children oral stories during our downtime and I also told stories to small groups of 3 to 4 children with books and props. But I had never told a story during group time without props. Having cared for this group of children for over a year, establishing relationships with them and aware of their abilities, I was now confident that I could tell an oral story during group time without props. I thought of *Abiyoyo*, an oral story also available in book form that I had told to young preschool children several years ago. This story was memorable because I had told the story to both of my own children when they were preschoolers, and now I was ready to tell it to children much younger than my sons were at that time. I hoped my current group of children would enjoy it as much as my boys.

Abiyoyo is an old African tale made popular by Pete Seeger (1986). It is the story of a little boy who made "loud noise" with his ukulele, which bothered the townspeople; his father, the trickster magician; and their cultural tradition of telling stories about the giants that lived a long time ago. One of the giants they told stories about was named Abiyoyo, who had messy hair, long finger nails, and stinky feet, and most frightening of all, he was as tall as a tree and could eat sheep in one gulp. When Abiyoyo appears, the little boy gets in a show as to how he and his father can make Abiyoyo disappear.

To refamiliarize myself with the details of the story, I reread it and memorized some of the more captivating moments. I thought of parts of the story where I could get the children to physically engage with the story and parts where I could pause and ask the children to predict what might happen next. I began to tell the story with a very soft voice to which the children immediately reacted by paying close attention, concentrating on what I was saying. I then quickly moved into a louder voice as I described the little boy playing his ukulele and the reaction of the townspeople. At one point, I saw that the children were beginning to lose interest, so I asked them to join in with me, and they played their air ukulele and sang "clink clank clunk." When the father in the story takes out his magic wand, I asked the children to say "zoop zoop" with me as they waved their pretend wands in the air, and when the little boy runs toward Abiyoyo, they patted their legs to make the sound of little feet running quickly. I changed some challenging vocabulary such as *ostracized* and used this explanation instead: "The people told the little boy and his papa to go away since they needed space." We had discussed the need for "space" earlier that day and so it fit well here. Later, when I talked about the townspeople who were scared of Abiyoyo and ran away, the children practiced their own scared expressions.

I had never considered telling this story to such young children because it was long and had so many challenging concepts. However, the combination of my storytelling without props and making the story interactive helped introduce new vocabulary and provoked self-expression. As I continued to tell the story over the next few weeks, I used more sophisticated language, such as when the little boy and his papa were "ostracized." I also included the word *disappear* for when the magician uses his magic wand, as opposed to saying simply "zoop zoop" to make things go away. Retelling the story several times allowed me to gradually scaffold the children's exposure to and understanding of complex vocabulary (for further discussion on teacher storytelling with older children, see Chapter 4 in this volume).

I recently went for a walk outside our center with the children, and I pointed out the various colorful flowers and tall trees. Some of the children repeated what I was saying, but 25-month-old Alex looked up at me and said, "Eh-ka [Erica], Abiyoyo, tall tree." I agreed that Abiyoyo was as tall as a tree. Alex said to me, "Abiyoyo eat sheep, no Alex," cupped his hand and pretended to gulp his empty hand. I then used Alex's association of Abiyoyo with the trees to ask everyone to look around for things that Abiyoyo would eat. This was a wonderful child-initiated opportunity for me to extend our Abiyoyo storytelling.

GENA'S STORY

As I moved through the year with the 2- to 3-year-olds in my classroom, I found that stories often promoted children's spoken language, and conversations about our book sharing were lengthier and more focused than other conversations in the classroom. In this section, I discuss the way book sharing with young children encouraged their use of language and facilitated their development of comprehension. In the often spontaneous moments in our book sharing, the children and I were almost always equal participants in making meaning out of the stories and pictures. I found that our book sharing experiences eventually moved the children from using language primarily to express their needs to having original conversations with peers and adults. Since young children are at the beginning of learning language and conversing with peers, this transition toward conversation was not easy.

So I began to audiotape some of our book exchanges, hoping to examine more closely the relationship between book sharing experiences and the art of conversation with young preschoolers. I found that our reading together not only encouraged the children to talk with one another, but it also gave them an opportunity to construct meaning together as they tried to understand new and familiar stories. I also found three factors that facilitated this process: 1) scaffolding between children and adults, 2) connecting personal experiences, and 3) providing prompts. I now use excerpts from three conversations to discuss how these elements worked.

One of the early conversations between Anthony (3.4 years old), Sarah (3.1 years old), and me lasted 15 minutes. The conversation unfolded as I read *The Earth and I* (Asch, 1994), an unfamiliar story about a boy describing his feelings for the Earth. As I read the one-sentence per page text, we stopped to ask each other questions about the pictures, and the talk evolved into a conversation about the children's personal experiences and interpretations.

The second exchange involved Seth (3.9 years old), Anthony, and me and *Ella Sarah Gets Dressed* (Chodos-Irvine, 2003). The conversation lasted for 7 minutes and took place before I began reading, as the boys initiated looking at the book's cover and identifying the letters in the title.

The third exchange was the shortest at 3 minutes, and involved Seth and me. Seth initiated our collaboration by saying that he wanted to read the familiar book *Chugga Chugga Choo Choo* (Lewis, 1999) to me, and then quickly asked me to read it to him instead. Ultimately, we retold the story together as Seth turned the pages at the appropriate times. I also read the beginning of each page and Seth finished by completing the story's rhyming text.

Scaffolding and Personal Story Connections

The children were becoming more interested in engaging with one another, so they benefited from hearing not just from their teacher, but from peers as well. In the following two excerpts from the first conversation between Sarah, Anthony, and me, peer collaboration and adult-child scaffolding strenghten pesonal connections to *The Earth and I.*

> *Anthony:* Is that also the planet? (pointing to the cover of the book)
> *Gena:* This is called *The Earth and I*, and yes, the Earth *is* a planet.
> *Anthony and Sarah:* Yeah.
> *Anthony:* It is called The Earth and I and the Earth *is* a planet.
> *Sarah:* Planets fly around like this. (moving her arm in a circular motion)
> *Gena:* They fly in the universe—kind of float around up there.
> *Anthony:* Yeah, and rocket ships.

As we examined the illustration of the Earth, Sarah extended my planet explanation by telling and showing how planets move, which prompted me to use the word *universe*, which in turn prompted Anthony to contribute his knowledge of rocket ships to our discussion. Without the time and opportunity for mutual collaboration, Anthony may not have grasped the new idea of the Earth as a planet before we moved on with the reading.

> *Gena:* What's happening with the Earth now?
> *Sarah:* It's raining.
> *Gena:* What else is happening? What are these things?
> *Sarah:* Thunder—lightning. (correcting herself)
> *Gena:* Lightning bolts—what else happens when there's lightning?
> *Sarah:* BOOM-BOOM—that is thunder! When thunder comes next to your house, really loud, and it even might could scare you.

Gena: Yes, it could even scare you if it's very loud.

Sarah: I don't like it.

Anthony: And monsters? Or Power Rangers? I mean bears, or I mean Power Rangers, or I mean monsters come in? (asking Sarah)

Gena: Does that happen when there's thunder?

Sarah: Um, actually um, because I'm a Power Ranger and Superman—I have lots and lots of Superman powers, and I can fight anything away that is scary.

Anthony: Yeah, because you have a light saber and a gun and a sword at your house.

Sarah: Yeah, I have a weapon and a sword. That will fight them really badly.

Gena: Does that make you feel safe?

Sarah: Yeah. But I can only do it.

Anthony directed his question "And monsters? Or Power Rangers?" to Sarah as he tried to relate to the way she felt about thunder. I then tried to help Sarah understand what I thought Anthony was asking her, and then this side conversation took a sharp turn as Sarah and Anthony reclaimed their power—"I'm a Power Ranger and Superman." I realized at that point that they were getting the reinforcement they needed from each other, and my teacher scaffold was not needed in that part of the conversation.

In another scaffolding example, Seth, Anthony, and I looked at the cover of *Ella Sarah Gets Dressed*, and the boys excitedly pointed out letters in the book's title (see Figure 1.1).

Anthony: That's Ella Sarah. Look, that have an "A" like "Anthony." And another "A" for "Anthony."'

Gena: Yes, she has some A's in her name like you do.

Seth: And another A!

Anthony: And another A. . . .Well, there's three A's. One, two, three.

Gena: What else do you see?

Anthony: Is that an A? (pointing to a letter)

Gena: That's an S.

Anthony: And what is this?

Seth: T . . . T for Tom!

Gena: Yeah, T, like in your dad's name.

Seth: T for Tom, Anthony.

Gena: Do you know what that letter is?

Figure 1.1. Seth, Anthony, and Gena Look at *Ella Sarah Gets Dressed*

Anthony: No.
Seth: E . . . for eagle.
Anthony: What is this?
Gena: What *is* that one? Do you know, Seth?
Seth: D.
Anthony: For dragon. What's this?
Seth: E—another E!
Anthony: Two Es.
Seth: Three Es!
Anthony: One, two, three Es.

I remember feeling that this conversation flowed well, and that it felt like the children were motivated to participate with very minimal prompting from me. My role was certainly supportive, and not leading. For example, Seth answered his friend's question quickly ("T for Tom") and then reiterated his answer two lines later to be sure that Anthony had understood. The children took on the teacher role, as also seen when Anthony extended Seth's identification of the letter "d" by attaching the word *dragon*.

Our book sharing often involves spontaneously sharing a personal anecdote related to the material. This happens for the children when a storyline or picture sparks a memory of personal experience, and it happens for me when I see an opportunity to make new information more meaningful for the children in a personal way. For instance, in my discussion of *The Earth and I* with Sarah and Anthony, the children pretended to eat when they saw an illustration of people eating in the story. I then connected the children's action with an appreciation for the fact that the Earth grows food that we can eat. In an attempt to make it more concrete, I also referred to food items that Sarah and Anthony had seen me eating earlier that day.

> *Gena:* What do you think this child's eating?
> *Sarah:* I don't know.
> *Gena:* Something from the Earth, if the Earth is helping him grow.
>   Maybe these vegetables that just grew out of the Earth. . . .
>   Maybe he raked out the vegetables and he made it into food
>   that he could eat?
> *Anthony:* Maybe pasta, he made it into.
> *Gena:* Maybe . . . there are some fruits and vegetables that grow
>   right out of the Earth that we can eat right away. Like the
>   tomatoes that I had today in my lunch, and the cucumbers.
>   You don't even have to cook those things, you can just eat
>   them. You take them out of the Earth, you wash them off, and
>   you can eat them. What do you think?
> *Anthony:* I didn't know that!

The following section is from the same conversation. I related the actions of the child in the story to a personal experience the children had that morning when we left the center on a walk and encountered a tree, much larger than those found in the center's yard, which the children enjoyed climbing on.

> *Gena:* Oh, what's he doing here?
> *Anthony:* Sitting on that tree.
> *Gena:* Did you guys do that today? Do you remember when we
>   went on our walk and we found a climbing tree?

Anthony: Yeah, and I sat on it. Yeah, and I put my legs between . . .
Gena: The branches?
Anthony: Yeah.
Gena: How lucky that we found that climbing tree—that the Earth
    let that tree grow so big for us! You guys were able to climb on
    it. . . . Can you climb on very small trees? (They shake their
    heads.) No, we have to wait until they're so strong and big and
    healthy, after they've grown a lot.
Sarah: Yeah, because if they are really strong and they can hold
    big kids. That means that the Earth made them grow, grow,
    grow, grow. . . .

In this instance, we used the book as a prompt for the children to recall their own experience relating to this part of the story. These positive
social experiences around shared reading and discussion will have a lasting influence on the children's interest in talking and learning about their
world through story.

Providing Prompts

I find it valuable to ask open-ended questions and provide prompts
that allow children to become successful story discussants. For example,
as we continued to read *The Earth and I*, I pointed to a part of the picture
that depicts swirling gusts of wind, and asked Anthony and Sarah if they
recognized the object. Anthony surprised me by saying, "I don't know.
What does that rope do?" I then realized what was potentially confusing
about the picture—he had recognized the gusts of wind as ropes. Having
focused on this small aspect of the page, Anthony was not able to see the
"big picture," which included leaves blown around. After trying to explain what Anthony saw, I extended his point by also talking about what
happens when the wind blows.

I also ask questions based on an "interactional model of question sequencing" (Vander Woude & Barton, 2003, p. 267) that involves reiterat-
ing or altering the questions I ask children during our reading discussions
to help them become successful conversants. I try to rephrase or make my
question "easier" or more developmentally appropriate to keep the flow
and content of our conversation going. For example, with Anthony and
Sarah, I did not ask a second, more specific question until my first one
was met with several seconds of silence from the children. At that moment, I pointed to the lightning bolts in the picture of *The Earth and I* to
offer a more specific visual prompt.

Gena: What else is happening? What are these things?
Sarah: Thunder—lightning. (correcting herself)

And later in the same conversation:

Gena: (reading) "We play together in my backyard." What's this
    child doing with the Earth in his backyard? Using his shovel
    to . . .
Anthony: Dig, dig, dig, dig, dig . . . .

I waited several seconds after asking the first question in each of the
excerpts, and then, realizing that Sarah and Anthony were still thinking,
I offered a "hint" ("Using his shovel to . . . ") to provide more information
and help the children continue our conversation.

In another example, Seth and I retold the story depicted in *Chugga
Chugga Choo Choo.* Here, I began each sentence and, trusting that Seth had
a strong memory for this familiar story, I allowed time for him to finish
the rhyme.

Seth: I only can read a little bit, not a lot.
Gena: Okay, read as much as you can. I'd love to hear it.
Seth: I want you to read.
Gena: What's this book about? "Chugga chugga choo choo.
    Whistle . . ."
Seth: ". . . blowing—whoo whoo."
Gena: "Hurry, hurry, load . . ."
Seth: ". . . the freight. To the city, can't be late."
Seth: I wonder what's in those boxes?
Gena: Anything could be in there—maybe some food or clothes.
Seth: Or maybe a "jack-in-the-box."
Gena: Yeah. "Through the country, on the . . ."
Seth: ". . . loose."
Gena: "Engine black, and . . ."
Seth: ". . . red caboose."

We both felt a sense of accomplishment when we finished the book
together, especially because Seth had initially expressed interest in "reading" the story to me, but then had second thoughts, perhaps doubting his
ability to retell the entire story on his own. With my prompting, he set
a good pace with his page-turning and we successfully "read" the book
together. In *The Read-Aloud Handbook* (Trelease, 2001), Trelease recognizes
the importance of this strategy by instructing readers "during repeat read-

ings of a predictable book, to occasionally stop at one of the key words or phrases and allow the listener to provide the word" (p. 99). The amount of control that Seth had in our retelling also prompted him to voice his own curiosities as he asked, "I wonder what's in those boxes." Barrett-Dragan (2001) discusses the value of reflecting and retelling activities as strategies for developing comprehension and memory, "helping children understand how stories are structured and organized, how story language works, and how to use language creatively" (p. 82).

CONCLUSION

Beginning in infancy, secure relationships are central to the quality of children's early social and linguistic experiences with story. Erica's section describes the development of these relationships, and the unique way that she saw receptive and expressive language grow through the sharing of stories. For example, the intimate connection she made with Mary helped sustain Mary's attraction to stories over time, and provided her with a foundation for future language and literacy interests around story.

As children grow, book sharing is one way to scaffold children's efforts to come to their own conclusions and begin to construct meaning by asking questions and offering prompts to further our conversations. Gena's section describes her experiences sharing stories with slightly older children, and the ways stories encourage more in-depth conversations and complex use of language and concepts. For example, Anthony and Seth promoted one another's understanding of the way letters represent the names of people and objects. Oral stories and books shared in an informal way can draw children into the experience of story characters, encouraging them to connect their own experiences and therefore make the story more personally meaningful. This happened, for instance, with Sarah and Anthony as they discussed thunder and lightning, which they then connected to what scares *them* and how they work through their fears.

We have found that daily, consistent use of stories in the classroom enriches infants' and toddlers' exposure to and interest in varied forms of language and literacy. As teachers of young children, we also have the social and developmental challenge of helping children navigate conversations with peers and adults. This process, when enriched by rich stories and rhymes, becomes wonderfully multifaceted, and influences young children's linguistic, social, and cognitive growth. At the heart of this linking of language and stories are close, personal relationships between children and their caregivers, an intimate physical setting, and unhurried time to allow for participation and contemplation.

REFERENCES

Allen, A. (2000). *What is it?* San Diego: WS Publishing.

Asch, F. (1994). *The Earth and I.* San Diego: Harcourt Brace.

Barrett-Dragan, P. (2001). *Literacy from day one.* Portsmouth, NH: Heinemann.

Chodos-Irvine, M. (2003). *Ella Sarah gets dressed.* San Diego: Harcourt Brace.

Lewis, K. (1999). *Chugga chugga choo choo.* New York: Hyperion Books for Children.

Seeger, P. (1986). *Abiyoyo.* New York: Macmillan.

Trapani, I. (1997). *Twinkle, twinkle little star.* Watertown, MA: Charlesbridge Publishing.

Trelease, J. (2001). *The read-aloud handbook* (5th ed.). New York: Penguin Books.

Vander Woude, J., & Barton, E. (2003). Interactional sequences in shared book-reading between parents and children with histories of language delay. *Journal of Early Childhood Literacy, 3 (3),* 249–273.

Chapter 2

Using Story Drama with Young Preschoolers

TODD WANERMAN

Todd Wanerman is a veteran preschool teacher whose teaching interests focus
on the inclusion of special needs children and the value of stories and story drama
for toddlers and preschoolers. Todd is also interested in the use of technology to
improve teachers' observing and understanding of children's learning. Todd is a
student in the M.A. in Early Childhood Education program at San Francisco State
University.

Heidi, a 2-year-old, asks me to read *The Three Little Pigs*, a favorite in the
classroom for several weeks. "Climb up in the loft this time," I suggest. "I'll
be the wolf and you be the pigs." As many as seven more children join in
as I hold up the book while reading the simple text. Some children bring
brightly colored plastic hammers from the toolbox and pound away at
the loft, building the houses. I knock on the side of the loft and call out,
"Little Pig, Little Pig, let me come in!" "No!" most of the children cry out, and
some just scream. I reply, "The book says . . . 'not by the hair on my . . .'"
"Chinny chin chin!," chorus the children. When we reach the page in the
book where the third pig builds a fire under the chimney, I climb into the
loft, and then jump and read, "the Big Bad Wolf ran down the road and the
three little pigs never saw him again." I encourage the "pigs" to celebrate
together with high fives. "Do it again!" the children insist.

STORY DRAMA FOR TODDLERS

MANY TALENTED AND creative teachers such as Vivian Paley (1981,
1990) and Bev Bos (2007) have developed exciting ways to
help young children use imaginative play and stories to ad-

27

vance their language, social, emotional, and cognitive capacities. These approaches share much in common—a respect for children's ideas and words, a shared sense of joy and creativity around storytelling, a dedication to using structured dramatic play to deepen the bonds of the classroom community, and a focus on children as emerging storytellers and writers. These approaches also tend to focus on children in the later preschool or kindergarten years. Young preschoolers (ages 2–3), though, have not been the focus of story drama discussions, as some developmental beliefs suggest that this kind of curriculum is beyond their reach—children in this age group do not yet engage in pretend play, are not generally interested in organized social interaction, and their language skills are too immature.

In my work with 2- and 3-year-olds, however, I see threads of these capacities emerging all the time—a child "chases" a figurine of a man with a growling lion doll, another jumps on a plank and declares she is "skateboarding," pairs of children pretend to be "kitties" and charm the teacher into "feeding" them. These and other examples show toddlers' emerging abilities to use language, organize simple interactive play, and use symbols and representations. What they lack, compared to 4- or 5-year-olds, is a "script" to set up roles and actions and focus the play over an evolving set of steps.

In my teaching, I have found that using story books as a script for simple, teacher-facilitated group pretend play can be a very satisfying and effective experience for young preschoolers, and one that responds and promotes children's individual ideas and development. Story drama provides a developmental link between infants' sensory exploration of materials and the interactive pretend play of pre-kindergartners. Like Vivian Paley's story drama techniques, this toddler-age story drama practice fosters exploration and variation, honors children's contributions, and focuses on helping children find meaningful roles for themselves and with one another. But there are two main differences. First, story books form the working script, rather than children's story retellings or self-generated stories. Second, the teacher plays an active role in the drama with the children.

In my work, I see how young preschoolers are driven to acquire and use new language skills as a means of learning more satisfying ways to play. Story drama is a rewarding and effective way for focusing children's (and teachers') attention on how language can support the development of children's imaginative and social skills. To be sure, it must function under the umbrella of teachers' general emergent response to children's interests and ideas. But if we also tailor these activities to the unique personalities and interests of our children, we can use story drama to promote some very exciting language development.

STORY DRAMA—SOME BASIC COMPONENTS

Story drama is an ideal curriculum approach with young preschoolers because it is essentially simple—teachers encourage and support children to act out some of their favorite books. Underneath this basic premise, however, lie opportunities to promote a complex web of language skills—negotiating roles promotes self-advocacy and negotiation, exploring character and theme helps children articulate and explore emotions and gain self-knowledge, navigating the narrative thread develops sequential thinking, and discussing possible story outcomes involves abstract concepts and language. In order to promote these learning benefits to the fullest, we need to keep some basic components in mind.

Book Selection

There are many considerations about what to look for in selecting texts for story drama. I have found it most helpful to observe children's preferences and experiment with different stories. To maximize interest and satisfaction, I look for stories that feature and explore strong *affect* since toddlers are more connected to the emotions in a story than the ideas. Exploring children's imagination also challenges children to make cognitive and linguistic sense of emotional experience. Children are naturally attracted to stories with strong emotional content, as seen by the enduring popularity of fairy tales. "The Three Little Pigs" or "The Three Billy Goats Gruff" serve as symbols for young children's maturation and mastery over danger and fear. I do not shy away from negative emotions, as children benefit from exposure to and exploration of a wide range of emotions.

Rhythm, rhyme, and *repetition* in stories are also highly effective for helping children engage with an imaginative theme. Honig (2006) has pointed out that rhythm is a fundamental presence in children's development, from in utero to memorizing abstract academic concepts when children are older. Rhythm and rhyme form a scaffold for mastering scripts and character, and when combined with dialogue and verbal turn-taking, even the most repetitive texts support children's drama.

Visual Prompts and Music

Even when language acquisition is our goal, toddlers have very limited capacities for understanding spoken language without some form of support. We also know that children learn best when information is double-coded, or presented in more than one way. This is why story books form the backbone of toddler story drama curriculum. Pictures and text together help very young children understand the narrative and themes of story and give them a platform for enacting and expanding upon them. It is effective to make the fullest possible use of illustrations, flannel board shapes, overhead projections, and puppets to help children understand a story.

Similarly, music is processed in an area of the brain separate from language. Pairing text with music can form a powerful double-code for language and social development, since it literally sends stories into the brain through two portals. Many books are available on tape or CD with musical accompaniment and many songs can be transformed into stories.

Beyond the Book Corner

It is helpful not to limit children's story drama exploration to books or the book corner. Group music time can also provide an exciting and enticing forum, and chants, finger plays or favorite songs can also be transformed into collaborative performance. For example, 2-year-olds in our class often love to learn a simple Halloween rhyme during the fall:

> Five little pumpkins sitting on a gate
> A ghost came flying by
> "Ha ha ha, I'll take you home
> And make some pumpkin pie."

We first present the rhyme at group time by drawing on a dry-erase board as we chant, removing one pumpkin from the fence each time and adding one pie in the ghost's "cave." Later we use finger puppets or flannel board shapes to allow the children to re-enact the sequence on their own during free choice time. The children often like to read a book with a similar rhyme, 5 Little Pumpkins (Yaccarino, 1998). If the children remain interested, we set out five small chairs during group time and invite children to take turns being "pumpkins." All children who are interested can play the part of the "ghost" at once. This is a good example of balancing text structure with children's individual initiatives—we often act the chant out over several sessions to give everyone a chance to participate.

The teachers prompt the "pumpkins" in the art of affective response: "OK, pumpkin number 3, the ghost is coming for you. How would your face look?" We advise the ghosts in the often challenging task of waiting "offstage" until they "come flying by," entering and reciting the ghost's lines and gently leading one pumpkin at a time offstage. Children who do not choose to act out a role are given rhythm sticks and encouraged to provide another level of "text" by chanting and playing.

When children show especially high interest in a particular theme or story, I often give them other opportunities to explore it even further. We might use small houses and figurines to act out a story in the fine-motor realm in the play dough, sensory, or manipulative areas. Children and teachers sometimes collaborate at the art table to build masks, costumes, or props, or even a large puppet of a Big Bad Wolf or Abiyoyo. Scissor or marker work at the writing area might also revolve around photocopies of pages from our current favorite book, and children can put several copied pages in sequence to make their own "book."

Engaging All Learners

When I make mindful use of stories and dramatic play to promote social and linguistic development, I try to engage and enable all kinds of learners to work together and take "center stage." I do so by observing all the children and make careful note of each child's preferences. I make a point of building story drama around the favorite books, spaces, and play styles of many different children. Since stories are so universally prized by young preschoolers, virtually every student has favorites that can serve as the impetus for story drama.

But what about young children with very little expressive language? Or those who seem happy to play by themselves with a train set all day? Or those who explore by staying on the move—running, climbing, and jumping? Or those with specific learning differences or challenges? And should we even try to lead young preschoolers into group dramatic play experiences if they don't seem ready? While we certainly must honor each child's unique style and pace, and while many toddlers do simply need more time than others to develop an interest in dramatic play, our challenge is to help all children find meaningful and connected places in the group. As groups form around story drama, we can then look for particular ways to help each child feel empowered and connected to the emerging classroom community.

How, then, can we use stories to draw in diverse learners and maximize their individual experiences? Leila, for instance, enjoyed school as a 2-year-old, but rarely spoke and played mostly on her own. In October of her second school year, her classmates became preoccupied with a picture book entitled *Big Pumpkin* (Silverman & Schindler, 1995), a Halloween-themed adaptation of the classic folk tale in which a succession of people—a witch, a ghost, a vampire, a mummy, and a bat—try to pull a large vegetable from the ground. My co-teachers and I had tied a green rope to a large pumpkin, and used a recording of the book rendered as a song to provide a framework for re-enactment. Although Leila watched her friends closely as they joined the teachers in acting out the story, she emphatically refused the teachers' invitation to join in the play, and moved to the farthest point in the room whenever the "mummy" appeared.

My co-teacher eventually asked Leila if she would hold the book for the children to follow along. She agreed. For two class sessions, in front of her friends and with the book facing away from her, Leila turned the pages at the sound of the beep. This role provided Leila with a comfortable entry into play and mitigated her fear of the fantasy. She kept the book clutched in her hands as the teachers modeled the characters' actions and feelings and facilitated discussions about each monster, why they looked like they did, whether they were "mean" or "nice," and what they wanted.

By the eighth or ninth day of dramatizing the story, as teachers we had reduced our level of participation since the children had become so adept and independent in the drama. But just before clean-up time, I noticed that, all on her own, Natalie, one of the most confident and engaged players, held the book and Leila was in the middle of the line, holding the green rope and playing the part of the mummy.

Manageable Steps

Just as it helps children to break cognitive or motor challenges down into manageable steps, it helped Leila to engage with peers when we helped her break down the process into smaller steps. This required us to be patient and give her time simply to observe. When we saw cues that she was ready—such as when she observed the play more and more closely—we offered her a transitional role, one that did not force her into the middle of the action but was nonetheless a real and meaningful job that enabled her to find her way into the play at her own pace.

Language Beyond Words

Leila did not utter a word—from the text or otherwise—in this vignette, and using language with her peers remained an ongoing learning process for her long after this play episode took place. The scripted interaction provided by the book, however, helped her engage with peers. Just as play provides a structure for children to communicate with one another, language in turn helps children advance their play skills. The language need not play the same role—or, in Leila's case, a particularly visible role—every time to have a positive impact on a child's advancing language and social skills. Today, however, having built confidence and connections with her peers, in part with help from books, Leila has a major "say" in her peer group.

The Sensory Perspective

Even in the realm of dramatic play, children not only engage with all their senses, but their individual comfort levels and sensitivity guide their participation. When thinking of ways to extend or individualize story drama, I keep some basic questions in mind about each child: How does this child like to be approached? What kind of physical connections does she seek out or avoid? How does she most naturally express herself—verbally, physically, musically, or otherwise?

Understanding how children engage with the world in terms of their sensory integration and response not only helps teachers understand how and when to support their story drama participation, but also what kind of participation to support. One child might prefer to talk about the text with a teacher and read it together before doing anything physical. Another might want just the opposite—to engage with the story through moving and physically interacting with others before being ready to explore words and ideas. Some may need to take on the loud, aggressive voice of the troll or the monster. Others may be easily overwhelmed by loud, scary elements and need to keep some distance at first.

The sensory perspective also gives us a wider range of ideas for structuring story drama play. Simple experiences such as hugging, climbing, hanging, lifting, or stretching can adjust a child's (or a group's) receptivity and arousal to maximize their social and language potential. We often act out William Steig's *Pete's a Pizza* (2003) because the "father" (played by a teacher with as many "co-parents" from the group as are inclined) puts the "child" (again, as many as are interested) through a very toning regime of sensory experiences as we make them into "pizzas."

FROM PAGE TO STAGE—STORY DRAMA IN FIVE BASIC STEPS

There is, of course, no one right formula for helping children act out stories. One of the great strengths of this approach is its simplicity and its flexibility. But over many years of acting out stories with toddlers and allowing for variation, I regularly follow these basic steps:

Step 1: Read and Re-Read Children's Favorite Books

Effective story drama for young preschoolers starts with teachers providing a rich and central place for stories in the classroom. I begin by considering how and when stories are presented to very young children as they begin school. Do I share my love of books and stories and read them often? Do I incorporate books and storytelling into other areas of the classroom? Above all, do I pay mindful attention to which particular books individuals and groups in the classroom love and request often? I choose a book for the children to act out if they have wanted me to read it repeatedly. I make sure that the children are very familiar with the text and have an ongoing interest as a foundation for turning the story into play.

Step 2: Use the Story as a Strong Scaffold

As teachers we can, in the classic Vygotskian (1967) sense, set the process of language and play learning in motion by first building a very sturdy scaffold. Texts as scripts for play naturally fit this role. Just as physical development progresses from gross motor to fine, children's engagement with stories and dramatic play progresses from simple to complex.

"The Three Billy Goats Gruff" is a perennial favorite story drama text among children in my classes, and offers an excellent example of how books can provide a structure for drama. First, the characters are clearly drawn and contrasted. Many children inevitably want to play the role of the third goat, since he uses his superior size and power to defeat the troll. But some children find that they are not quite ready to take on a monster, and opt to play the first goat, who gets an easy pass over the bridge. Still others are attracted to exploring the aggression and intensity of the troll. Second, the plot is laid out in a clear sequence. First one thing happens, then the next, and so on. Third, the action takes place in a clearly defined place—a bridge over a river. Almost anything can be used to build a bridge, which offers lots of opportunities for heavy pulling, lifting, and pushing as a means of getting organized together. The setting gives children clear cues where to be in physical relation to one another—the trolls hide under the bridge, while the goats trip trap over the top. And finally, the story is infused with rhythm and repetition. Children and teachers often like to use shakers or drums to create the constant "trip trap, trip trap" of the goats' hooves. As each goat crosses the bridge, they engage in the same dialogue and action as before, though with a slight but significant variation at the end.

Keeping the importance of visual prompts in mind, I hold the book up so children can follow along as I engage in the play. I also focus on dialogue as a means for the children to act and interact. It is this process of giving children a voice and actions that promotes rich language development.

Step 3: Play a Role Yourself

Since very young children learn through observing and playing with adults, I initiate the story drama process by playing a part myself. In this way, I model and structure the children's engagement, and I can keep the story moving even while helping children incorporate questions and discussion. When acting out stories with children, I focus on representing affect through language, actions, and tone and expression, but not in an overpowering, intimidating, or insincere way. When a story contains a particularly frightening or unsympathetic character, children often prefer to have the teacher take on this role. Pete Seeger's *Abiyoyo* (1994) has fascinated generations of toddlers in our program despite the fact that the title character, a giant who almost devours an entire town, scares most children. When I take on the role of the giant, and help guide the children through the story's plot of making me dance until I fall down on the ground and then making me disappear, I also model a sequence of feelings from angry to charmed to exhausted and show the children a manageable way to master fear.

Nicolopoulou and Richner (2007) discuss how teachers tend to focus on the sequencing potential of narrative when engaging in story play with children, but that as a result, the concept of character is underexplored. Besides the negotiating of roles, I also help children explore the attributes, motives, and feelings of characters as play moves along. Sensitivity to a range of characters makes story drama appealing and accessible to different kinds of learners.

Step 4: Focus on Interaction

Story drama offers a structure for children to learn to interact verbally and socially. We want to find ways to help children use dialogue and actions in the story as the focus for collaboration. As I guide young children in the early stages of acting out stories, I focus on ways to work together: building houses, hiding from the wolf together, putting on the pot of soup, and above all chanting "Not by the hair of my chinny chin chin!" and singing "Who's afraid of the Big Bad Wolf?" together.

Children often vie for the most prominent or "heroic" roles, such as the third little pig who outsmarts the wolf. I frequently encourage as many children as are interested to play a role together. Sometimes we have half a dozen "third" pigs in a performance. Turn-taking, however, allows children chances to try different roles and practice different dialogue. As children take on "bad guy" and "good guy" roles, or parent and child roles, they explore language, emotion, and social dynamics from multiple perspectives. Just as I want to encourage children to explore a range of emotions in play, I encourage them to explore a range of personas and to use fantasy to make sense of difficult or strong themes.

Step 5: Allow for Exploration and Variation

This is one of the more challenging, yet also valuable, aspects of acting out stories with children. We can provide definition through scripts, but we must avoid silencing or stifling children's own ideas and responses. Recall how some of the children in the "Three Little Pigs" episode chose to engage simply by using toy tools to build houses. Again, using Vygotsky (1967) as a guide, we can envision a balance whereby the script plays a more prominent role when children are very young and inexperienced, and gradually becomes more flexible and discreet as they grow and gain skill.

Although children benefit from a clear structure at first, they will also find their own ideas fairly quickly. A duo of 3-year-olds in our program recently finished enacting "Three Little Pigs" by "rewriting" the ending. In their coda to the story, the wolf returns to the house of bricks six successive times, engaging in—but losing—different kinds of physical conflicts with the pigs. These child-generated revisions open up opportunities for us to write down children's words and foster their emerging storytelling and early dictation capacities as well.

FINALE—BUILDING THE STAGE

By the end of 2 years in our classroom, children regularly initiate and manage their own dramatic play, with limited and well-rehearsed support roles for the teachers. The play often begins not with a book but with the stage itself. Groups of children pull out the entire classroom supply of big blocks to create a stage. They discuss how to arrange the blocks so that "no one falls off." They rummage through dress-up clothes in the house corner and negotiate who will play what role and what one must wear. Teachers often help children write a "list" of children wishing to take a turn "doing their own show." The children tape the list to the wall near the stage. They choose friends to be in their show (or occasionally choose to do a solo performance). Others choose to be the "audience." They also pick out music to accompany the production.

When each "director" deems his or her production ready, the teachers remind the audience of the rules of language in a theater—specifically, no talking when the lights go down (a rule the children usually insist on from real experience). As lights are dimmed, a teacher or child will call out, "Ladies and gentlemen! Presenting 'The Princesses at the Ballet!'" or more often, simply, "Presenting 'Miranda's Show!'"

We work with children in our classroom for 2 years—our students are 2 years old when they enter and 4 when they move on. As the examples in this chapter show, the ultimate goal of teachers supporting scripted dramatic play is to gradually enable children to take the lead in organizing and running the show. The structure provided by both teachers and books helps the children learn to link story language, social interaction, and dramatic play. But, as with so many supported kinds of play with young preschoolers, the most important teacher skill in this process is to watch for signs that children internalize some of these elements, and then begin to pull back and take down the scaffold.

As we see in Vivian Paley's work, children continue to use scripts and books in their play with each passing year. But by the time they are 4 years old, most children have taken ownership over both language and play, and they explore their own ideas for language and story. Often, they start to use language to dictate and "write" their own stories or retell favorites (see, e.g., in this volume, Chapters 9 and 10). Story drama promotes key connections between language, interaction, and dramatic play. The books act as the skeletal frame upon which children build their group dynamic and identity (not to mention early "reading" and "writing" experiences), and their habits of working together. As children grow, the skeletal frame remains at the center of their experience, but becomes submerged in the body of the group's play. We see in all kinds of dramatic play with older children how acting out books has helped them develop their own skills to get together, choose roles, make up a setting and a sequence of pretend actions, and evoke emotions. When you notice that the children no longer rely on you to guide them through imaginative play with a book in your hand, you will know that your practice of story drama has been a success.

REFERENCES

Bos, B. (2007). Storytelling workshop—National Association for the Education of Young Children. Retrieved July 21, 2008, from http://www.turnthepage.com/upload/528.pdf

Honig, A. S. (2006). Babies boost skills by taking advantage of rhythm and rhyme. *Early Childhood Today, 21*(2), 18.

Nicolopoulou, A., & Richner, E. S. (2007). From actors to agents to persons: The development of character representation in young children's narratives. *Child Development, 78(2)*, 412–429.

Paley, V. G. (1981). *Wally's stories: Conversations in the kindergarten*. Cambridge, MA: Harvard University Press.

Paley, V. G. (1990). *The boy who would be a helicopter: The uses of storytelling in the classroom*. Cambridge, MA: Harvard University Press.

Seeger, P., & Hays, M. (1994). *Abiyoyo: Based on a South African lullaby and folktale*. New York: Simon and Schuster.

Silverman, E., & Schindler, S. D. (1995). *Big pumpkin*. New York: Simon and Schuster.

Steig, W. (2003). *Pete's a pizza*. New York: Harper Collins.

Vygotsky, L. S. (1967). Play and its role in the mental development of the child. *Soviet Psychology, 6*, 6–18.

Yaccarino, D. (1998). *Five little pumpkins*. New York: Harper Festival.

FOR FURTHER READING

Arnold, R., & Colburn, N. (2005). Encore! encore! There's a good reason why kids love to hear the same story over and over. *School Library Journal, 51* (4), 35.

Brownell, C., & Kopp, C. (Eds). (2007). *Socioemotional development in the toddler years*. New York: The Guilford Press.

Mathieson, K. (2005). *Social skills in the early years: Supporting social and behavioral learning*. London: Paul Chapman Publishing.

Paley, V. G. (1984). *Boys and girls: Superheroes in the doll corner*. Chicago: University of Chicago Press.

Singer, D., & Singer, J. (1990). *The house of make-believe: Children's play and the developing imagination*. Cambridge, MA: Harvard University Press.

Chapter 3

The Superhero Project: Language, Stories, and Critical Thinking

Patricia Sullivan

---

*Patricia Sullivan directs a family childcare in her home, and is interested in is-
sues of social justice and critical thinking for her young children. Patricia holds an
M.A. in Early Childhood Education from San Francisco State University, and is
also currently a part-time instructor in early childhood education at San Francisco
State.*

The role of the teacher is likewise never neutral, but a political project on
behalf of, or against, the interests of those they teach. . . . A critical perspective suggests that deliberate attempts to expose inequity in the classroom
and society need to become part of our everyday classroom life.
—Vivian Vasquez,
Negotiating Critical Literacies with Young Children (2004)

THE SUPERHERO PROJECT

THE DAY BEGAN as it always did—with a race to the dramatic play box.
The boys rushed to put on capes and utility belts. Amid the chaos of
finding costume parts and the frustration of trying to put them on,
they quickly created the back story . . . Joker has captured Robin. Monsters have invaded the Justice League headquarters. Wonder Woman is
missing. There's no time to waste. The world needs us!

Zeke (age 3) knew everything about Spider-Man. He knew his real
name, his alter ego's name, his profession, and could even mimic Spider-
Man's movements of shooting webs from his wrists. As in the comic story,

39

Zeke could spot a spider from 20 feet away, a hypervigilance directly related to the radioactive spider that caused the geeky Peter Parker to acquire his superpowers. Zeke wanted to *be* Spider-Man. If only he weren't so desperately afraid of spiders! Frannie (age 4), conversely, didn't know much about superheroes. She didn't identify with the world-renowned male characters, and typically sidelined herself during free play. Before her two female playmates left for kindergarten, the girls adorned themselves with beautiful gowns, jewels, and slippers while the boys battled the agents of evil. Without them, Frannie no longer participated in dramatic play and the ultra-feminine princess costumes lay unused at the bottom of the box.

> *Zeke:* I'm Spider-Man. TA DA! (Takes an action stance, feet apart, knees bent, arms outstretched. His brow furrowed as he sticks out his right hand and points it at the trees.) Swishhhhhhhh POW! (He pulls on the imaginary web to test its strength.)
> *Kevin:* I'm Batman! I need a cape! (He runs into the building to dig through the costume box for a Batman costume, and returns to get someone to help him put it on. He has everything except the utility belt, which we lost last Halloween.)
> *Josh:* I'm Superman! I have a cape, too! (Josh begins to fly around the yard with the cape his mother made. He carries the cape everywhere he goes.)
> *Patricia* (me): What about you, Frannie? Which superhero are you going to be?
> *Frannie:* I want to be Superman. (She is sad because Josh is already Superman.)
> *Zeke:* You can't be Superman! He's a boy!
> *Patricia:* That doesn't matter; we're just playing pretend anyway. But did you know that there are women superheroes, too?
> *Frannie:* I don't know their names.
> *Patricia:* Let's look in some of the books we have on superheroes and maybe we will find some that are girls and women.
> *Frannie:* I know! Elastic-girl! She's an Incredible!
> *Zeke:* Yeah! She can stretch really far and she's a girl AND a mommy!

Vivian Vasquez (2004) believes the best source for critical language and literacy projects involves children's play and, in particular, their life interests. As I observed my children's play, I became acutely aware of my family childcare's embarrassingly stereotypical costume assortment and was also intrigued by the children's attraction to people with extraordinary abilities. I wondered, "What was it about superheroes that they find so appealing?" As we became engrossed in the superhero project over the next several weeks, I found myself "using" this project to extend my children's conversational skills and understanding of story to think critically both with me and with one another.

Defining Characters, Superpowers, and Motivation

I began by asking the children to show me what superheroes do. They quickly put on the capes and masks and flew about the meadow behind our school. They pantomimed picking up really heavy things, jumping from tall buildings, shooting webs and swinging gracefully through the air, fighting invisible bad guys and saving people. I asked why superheroes do the things they do and they were quick to respond that "helping" was their job and responsibility. People with superpowers who didn't want to help others were bad guys. As they named their favorites and described their powers, I recorded their responses on the white board:

- Superhero: Special abilities
- Superman: Super strong, flees, hot rays from his eyes
- Batman: Good fighter, lots of cool gadgets, bat cave, utility belt, bat ropes, cape, airplane, motor cycle
- Wolverine: Big claws, gets hurt and gets better
- X-man: Gets other super people to help him
- Mr. Incredible: Super strong
- Elastic-girl (Ms. Incredible): Stretches into any shape

It became clear to the group that there was a significant variety in superpowers and that Batman, one of their favorites, has no superpowers at all. Batman is just a regular guy who wants to stop crazy criminals like Joker. But despite this realization, there was no question of his superhero status. I wondered, "If the type and degree of superpowers do not make a super hero, what is the most important characteristic?" So I asked the group, and everyone gave about the same response: superhero values demonstrated by a commitment to good works and good deeds. This deeper understanding of superheroes surprised me. I expected the children to focus on the cool uniforms, or that superheroes always win, or maybe their general popularity. But clearly, the children specifically identified with the characters' commitment, dedication, and ability to change the world for the better and save the day more than anything else.

Next, I asked the group a series of questions to clarify their connections with superheroes and to help them imagine themselves not only wearing the uniforms, but adopting some of the positive values they see in their favorite superheroes.

Superhero Survey

Question 1: Are girl superheroes as strong as boy superheroes?
Frannie (4 years old): Yes
Josh (4 years old): Yes
Zeke (3 years old): Yes
Kevin (3 years old): Yes

Question 2: What are the names of the female superheroes you know?
Frannie: Elastic-girl
Josh: None
Zeke: None
Kevin: None

Question 3: What superpowers would you have if you were a superhero?
Frannie: Fly and strength
Josh: Fly and strength
Zeke: Fly and strength
Kevin: Fly and strength

Question 4: Why do superheroes help people?
Frannie: They like it
Josh: They have to
Zeke: It's their job
Kevin: They just do

Question 5: What could you do to help others without superpowers?
Frannie: Help my mom
Josh: Take care of my sister
Zeke: Be nice
Kevin: Do good stuff

When asked what they could do to help others, even without superpowers, the children were initially puzzled. Sure, Batman could do it, but he's a grown-up with a whole lot of money. They had not considered their own personal powers to help others. As our brainstorming session progressed, the children became more and more eager and excited about listing ways they could help others. Initially, the list started with things around the house or at school that they can do:

Brainstorm List of Ways We Can Help Others

Sharing our toys
Holding hands to keep each other safe
Getting the baby's pacifier or holding the baby's bottle
Take care of animals
No throwing garbage on the ground
Pick up garbage and recycle
Stop kids from being mean to other kids
Invite other kids to play when they're new

It was now clear to everyone in the group that it wasn't necessary to have superpowers to help others. They then expanded their new realization to other favorite characters who also spend a lot of time helping others. We developed a new brainstorm list:

Characters Who Help Others But Who Don't Have Superpowers

Chicken Little
Dora
Thomas the Tank Engine
Sponge Bob Squarepants
Batman
Buzz Lightyear
The Little Engine That Could
Parents

Nearly everyone in the group named their parents as people who help others. We talked about the ways that parents help at home: making meals, reading stories at bedtime, and taking them to favorite places like the zoo. Parents also perform heroic acts outside the home and in the community when they go to work. With my help, we brainstormed a list of the occupations of the children's parents.

Vocation of Baby Steps Parents

Second-grade Teacher
Photographer
Textile Artist

Actor/Writer/Director
Carpenter
Hospital Administrator
Musician
Regional Sales Manager
Contractor
High School Teacher
General Manager of apartment complex

As we discussed the many ways that parents help others, such as not lit-
tering and being careful when they drive, I told them that one of the best
ways that parents help their community is by voting. The children had no
idea what I was talking about. So I wondered, "How can I explain voting
in a developmentally appropriate way? How can I help them understand
voting as an act of heroism?"

OUR FIELD TRIPS:
THE RANDALL MUSEUM AND THE COMIC BOOK STORE

In order to foster their disposition to take action against injustice, we want
them to experience how it feels to engage in group social action. . . . We
want them to experience the power of working for change.
—Pelo & Davidson,
That's Not Fair: A Teacher's Guide to Activism (2000)

Explaining the City Election

To extend the children's growing social and linguistic talents for talking and thinking about superheroes and relating superhero powers to
their lives, we turned our focus to the upcoming city election. Our school
is a polling place and every year, sometimes several times, we clean out
the garage and get ready for the neighborhood to come to our school to
vote. It is always an exciting time for the children. They are fascinated by
the voting process, and the machine that "eats" the ballots. On Election
Day the children like to sit on the grass outside the garage and watch the
grown-ups come and go with smiling faces and friendly waves.

When we first began to talk about voting, none of the children understood that to vote meant to choose or that voting is a personal power to
make choices in government, which can affect people's lives. So with the
election about a month away, I started by trying to describe the voting
process, which turned out to be a valuable language exercise for me as I

tried to put a difficult cognitive concept into developmentally appropriate language. I told the children that the adults were going to be voting for the next governor of the state of California. I explained that the governor is the leader of California and that the people of California vote to decide who our leader should be. On Election Day, voters mark a card with their choice for the leader and push it into the machine. Every neighborhood has a place where people go to choose who they want to lead California. At the end of the day, all the cards and machines are taken downtown to be counted and the person with the most votes becomes the leader of California.

The children understood the concept of people picking their leader, but had difficulty with the concept of "city" and the "state of California." Although some of the children could tell me the name of their city, most were confused about the boundaries. Zeke said, "I live in San Francisco!" But when I said that I also lived there, too, he frowned. "Only I live in San Francisco with my mommy and daddy," he insisted. It wasn't until later that I realized that Zeke believed the boundaries of San Francisco to be the exact dimensions of his apartment on Hayes Street.

Maps proved useless. Two-dimensional blobs of color have little significance for 3- and 4-year-olds. So I wondered, "How can I help the children see the whole city?" I decided to start with our building, and asked, "Look at our school from inside our classroom." They looked at the walls, the toys, and the furniture. "Can we see the whole building from this room?" I asked. Only Frannie understood that we couldn't see everything from inside. So we decided to go outside. "Can we see the building from the yard?" I asked. This time, everyone understood that we could only see the back of my house from the yard. We then walked to the front and had the same problem. Then we went for a walk around the block. We walked around all the houses and through the park meadow and back to the sidewalk on our street. When I asked, "Can you see our school?", they all pointed to the big palm tree on the front lawn and we counted how many houses we were from the end of the row. "All of these houses are in San Francisco," I said. We looked down the street. "We can't even see Zeke's house, and that's in San Francisco," I said. "Where could we go to see Zeke's house and maybe a few others all at once?"

Where Is the City?—Our Field Trip to the Randall Museum

The children said that we needed a high place to look out from, and so we took a field trip to the Randall Museum. The children brought their binoculars and we looked over San Francisco from the grassy courtyard of the Randall Museum, which is located on Twin Peaks and has a sweeping view of the heart of the city. From this western perspective, I pointed out the San Francisco Giants' baseball park, the tall buildings of downtown, and the surrounding neighborhoods. Each child tried to find their house among all the houses they saw. Looking at the cityscape gave the children a better understanding of perspective, and how our vantage point allowed us to see almost the whole city. I explained that San Francisco is only one city in California and that there are many more. Zeke and Kevin often took driving trips to Los Angeles and they both quickly told the other children that it "takes a long time" to get to Los Angeles. New questions then emerged about time and distance—how long it took for us to get to the playground or take a walk to the local grocery store. Even though they understood that both take a long time, it clearly took much longer to get to Los Angeles. Since we could not see Los Angeles from our Randall Museum lookout, the children seemed to reason, then Los Angeles must be too far away. But Los Angeles was still part of California, and so California must be pretty big.

Do Superheroes Vote?—Our Field Trip to the Comic Book Store

We got back into the van for our second stop before heading back to school. I promised Frannie that we would go to the comic bookstore to look for pictures of female superheroes. I wanted pictures to put in the classroom to give her a visual image of powerful female superheroes to help her join the boys in their superhero play.

We wasted no time getting to the superhero section, and there were books on Superman, Batman, and Pokémon. While they looked at the covers of the comic books, I saw the poster rack and quickly wrote down the numbers of the posters of superheroes. There were only two females in the group of 10, and so we asked the store owner for one of each female superhero poster.

"Do you think superheroes vote?" I asked Frannie. I wanted to build on her understanding of heroism without superpowers.

"How does voting help others?" Frannie asked me. I described some of the things that people vote for in elections: leadership, choosing or changing the way things are done, and special projects such as building bridges and making parks.

We ended up buying a few posters, and I also purchased a book of superhero women in the hopes of balancing out the overall number of pictures of male and female superheroes. Back at our school, I put the posters up on the walls. The children stood back to look. The posters were in brilliant color and as large as life: Superman, Batman, Spider-Man, Wonder Woman, the Justice League, Supergirl, and She-Hulk, posed like Rosie the Riveter.

"Do superheroes vote?" I asked the children, but the children still looked puzzled. So I explained that voting is a great way to help others. After some discussion, we made a banner for the parents to explain our new posters and our new understanding of what it means to be heroic. I read *Duck for President* (Cronin & Lewin, 2004) and *Click, Clack, Moo* (Cronin & Lewin, 2005) to explain the process of voting, but the concept of voting as helping others still remained too abstract for the children. I frustrated and out of ideas, I asked a few teacher friends for advice. One suggestion was that we hold our own elections, complete with written ballots and a ballot box. Instead of trying to explain the state election, this would help us focus on the election process and give them a chance to vote on things that were important to the children at school.

The next day we got right to work. We had been informally voting on the lunch and snack menu since the last election. Now the children all listed their favorite foods and we made a pictorial ballot. On Election Day, the children voted for their favorites and we tallied the votes. The excitement was palpable as the results were announced. Pizza, French fries, and rice were the big winners.

CRITICAL THINKING AS CRITICAL STORIES OF OUR LEARNING

In teaching critical thinking with young children, we have an obligation to help children learn to think, find answers to questions, and explore beyond the boundaries of their personal experience. We need to promote meaningful educational experiences that help to develop critical thinking skills to make informed choices. Stories play an important role in this process, as shown in our journey in understanding more about superheroes and connecting them to our lives.

In our current global renaissance, our children must be prepared for a future that relies on creativity and innovation, which are not skills acquired through memorization, rote learning, or scripted curricula. In my childcare setting, our critical thinking and conversations foster ongoing stories about social justice, how the world works (and doesn't), and how we can make changes. Our projects, like the superhero project, develop as we play in the sandbox, take a nature walk, or talk over lunch.

The ideas spring from the children's interactions, and in turn I support and extend their ideas through group brainstorming, vocabulary development, developmentally appropriate explanations of difficult concepts, field trips, brainstorms, and surveys. When I first hear an idea or interest with the potential for real traction and mileage, I write it down quickly and get my mini audiocassette recorder to interview the children before they forget what they said. It is my role as teacher to find ways for each child to connect to a project in as many different ways as possible by adding texture and depth to the adventure.

After finishing the Superhero Project, I knew my children had made the connection between personal power and the power of their vote. I was pleased that after this project, every conversation with my students became a debate between their choices and mine. Several children also did not understand why I solicited their vote only occasionally; they wanted to vote on everything. Even as I explained to the group that sometimes adults *have* to make the decisions and that they would have to go along, even if they didn't agree, I still sensed their resistance. And though this was at times frustrating, it was a welcome sign, as it indicated the power of linking critical thinking, language, and stories for young children.

REFERENCES

Cronin, D., & Lewin, B. (2005). *Click, clack, moo: Cows that type.* New York: Simon & Schuster.

Cronin, D., & Lewin, B. (2004). *Duck for president.* New York: Simon & Schuster.

Pelo, A., & Davidson, F. (2000). *That's not fair!: A teacher's guide to activism with young children.* St. Paul, MN: Redleaf Press.

Vasquez, V. M. (2004). *Negotiating critical literacies with young children.* Mahwah, NJ: Lawrence Erlbaum Associates.

Chapter 4

Telling Stories and Learning to Tell Stories: Lessons from a Professional Storyteller

NADIA JABONETA

Nadia Jaboneta is a preschool teacher at Pacific Primary School and also Centro Las Olas in San Francisco. Nadia has taught toddlers and preschoolers for 10 years. She is also the mother of a 2-year-old. She received her M.A. in Early Childhood Education from San Francisco State University in 2008. She is interested in storytelling and children's early literacy learning.

When I was a child, I used to sit on my grandmother's lap and listen to her stories. I can still recall how I felt, how I was mesmerized by her words, how I became one with the story. As my Mami Lila told each tale, I saw myself as one of the protagonists. I knew the characters intimately. I understood how each one felt and what they were each experiencing. No matter how many times my grandmother told a story, I listened as if for the first time while repeating the lines I had learned by heart. I will always cherish these story moments that I shared with my grandmother.

D URING WEEKLY STORYTELLING sessions told by Olive Hackett-Shaughnessy (see Figure 4.1), a professional storyteller, in my preschool classroom, I closely observed the children, watching their reactions to Olive's words and gestures. I often found several children watching attentively as if storyteller and each child were the only two people in the classroom and the story was intended just for them. When I saw the intensity of their facial expressions, I remembered my grandmother's stories and I wondered if my students felt the same emotions. I wondered, "Were the storyteller's words transporting them into the story?" "Were the children also now part of her tale?"

As a teacher, my interest in storytelling started with Olive's work in my classroom and my children's love of her stories. When I first met Olive and listened to her stories, I experienced first-hand how much oral storytelling promotes a love for stories and for language. I wanted to learn more about the art of oral storytelling and how I could use it to foster children's language development. I had read *Wally's Stories* (Paley, 1981) and I was intrigued by the way that Vivian Paley supported and listened to her children's stories. I read more about oral storytelling (see, e.g., Barton & Booth, 1990; Cooper, 1993; Stadler & Ward, 2005), which helped me take a closer look at my experience working with a professional storyteller and my own role as a storyteller.

"WHO IS OLIVE?"–THE ROLE OF THE TELLER

One morning, we had a discussion about Olive and her storytelling in our classroom. There were four new children in our class who had not yet participated in our storytelling sessions, and I wanted to make sure to tell them about Olive before she arrived. I then asked the class, "Who is Olive?"

Arianna: A teller story.
Niko: He does stories to friends.
Isabella: She tells stories.
Marcelo: She's pretty.
Kathy: She's this big! (Puts her arms up)

The children helped introduce Olive to their peers in their own child-language. Olive had become a friend to most of the children and they were always excited when I announced, "Story time with Olive!" I am also enthused when Olive comes to tell stories. By closely observing Olive, I have learned several techniques in the art of oral storytelling:

- Eye contact (look at the children or audience)
- Posture (sit comfortably, face the audience, change posture according to the story characters)
- Animation (facial expressions and gestures)
- Tone of voice (change voice according to story characters)
- Facial expression (shift facial expression when switching characters or to show emotion)
- Awareness of the audience (sense the need to regain audience attention before continuing)

Figure 4.1. Olive Telling a Story

- Audience participation (repeat chants or refrains, use body movements, make sound effects)
- Props (objects or stuffed animals relating to the story)
- Songs, chants, refrains (before, during, and after storytelling as attention keepers)

In Olive's telling of "Sody Sallyraytus," a story from *Grandfather Tales* (Chase, 1948), Olive expertly incorporates these techniques. In Olive's version of "Sody Sallyraytus," a little squirrel saves the day when children are eaten by a big hungry bear. The squirrel proves that she can be strong, and that even a powerful bear can be helpless. Every time one of the characters crosses the bridge, Olive leads the children in singing "Sody, sody, sody sallyraytus. Sody, sody, sody sallyraytus" as they use two fingers running across an arm to enact their crossing the bridge. In addition to the musical refrains and recurring phrases, Olive is very animated and incorporates body movements while telling this story. Through these and other techniques, Olive keeps the children consistently involved throughout the storytelling session.

TELLER AS A MODEL OF ORAL LANGUAGE

Olive's role in the classroom is a model of powerful oral language teaching. Her stories provide children opportunities to repeat chants and phrases that enhance their language learning experiences (Isbell, 2002). The children in my classroom have grown to love Olive's stories, but "Molly Mouse" (Ferlatte, 1997) has, by far, become the classroom favorite. The children enjoy repeating the story's catchy refrain of "Abunde. Abunde. Abunde tara bunde hah!" Olive, in turn, appreciates the children's love for this story and tells it often. By tailoring each telling of a story, as in "Molly Mouse," to the characteristics of each group of children, Olive makes a personal connection with the children. Olive usually begins her storytelling sessions by continuing a chant she taught the children the week before or by reciting one of the children's favorite chants. During the process of participating in these meaningful experiences, the children develop more complex communication skills. For example, many children use their interest in these stories as a way to connect with their peers in conversations and interactions.

One of Olive's many stories is "How Raccoon Got His Mask" (Cooper, 1995). She first taught the children how to say the Seneca name for "raccoon," which is *"Djo-aah-gah"* and then began the story, "A long, long, long, long, long, long, long, long, long time ago, before raccoons had masks, they were still very tricky as they are now." "How Raccoon Got His Mask" is about a sneaky raccoon who steals corn and ruins the field of an old couple. After seeing his damaged cornfield, the old man says, "I will punish the one who did this!" This line always captures the children's attention as their eyes focus on Olive and they smile and laugh in anticipation of the unfolding plot. Olive continues the story and how the next night the raccoon sneaks into the field again to steal more corn. The children are "story insiders" and know that the old man is tricky, too. He has spread hot mustard on the corn while the raccoon was sleeping. The children lean forward as the tension builds. What will happen next? The burn of a mouthful of hot mustard shocks the raccoon. Olive twists her face, pretends to spit out that mustard. The children laugh. The raccoon then gets a handful of mud to put in his mouth and rubs his muddy paws around his teary eyes, which creates a mask effect. Olive then ends the story, "The Great Spirit then says to him 'Raccoon you will always wear this mask. That way all will know just how tricky you are.'"

After this storytelling session, a small group of children sat down to eat a snack. I overheard them talking about the story, and specifically about the raccoons. I joined the group and listened in as 3-year-olds Marcelo Arianna conversed:

Marcelo: I know how raccoon got his mask. My mom and dad left the garage open and the raccoons got in. My baby brother found them and scared them away. Then they put on a mask with their claws to sneak back in, but they ran away. That's how they got their mask.

Arianna: That's not how he got a mask! I saw it all in front of my house. The raccoon came with his family to steal my garbage. They wore masks so that they wouldn't get caught stealing. They made a big mess.

These and other "outside of storytelling time" conversations reveal the children's great interest in Olive's stories involving animals, particularly if it is an animal they know something about. Raccoons are well known around the city and it is very common to have a family of raccoons dig through household garbage at night when they think no one is around. In these kinds of conversations, spurred on by Olive's storytelling sessions, children's verbal communication skills are enhanced as they "use" story to share their understanding of the world around them.

"I'm a Mean Old Witch"—Story and Rhyme

I'm a mean old witch with my hat (point to head),
I ride my broom with my cat (put hand out like claws),
I have pointy shoes (point to shoes),
and my nose is too (point to nose),
You better watch out or I'll scare YOU! (loudly)

—Author Unknown

One October, Olive began her storytelling by introducing this rhyme. By request, Olive retold it several times with the children until they had memorized it. Throughout the day, I caught myself, my assistants, and the children chanting this rhyme. At one point, I quietly repeated the rhyme to myself. Isabella stopped what she was doing to correct me, "No! You said it wrong. Your shoes are pointy first, not your nose!" She was right. I had the poem mixed up. Isabella reminded me how "fresh" children's memories of stories and rhymes are in comparison to mine. The children quickly memorized the rhymes and chants as they became a part of our storytelling rituals.

The children also created their own rhymes based on Olive's telling of "I'm a Mean Old Witch." One day, while several children explored puzzles in the manipulative center one morning, Marcelo began to chant "I'm a Mean Old Witch." I soon realized that Marcelo's rhyme was not

Olive's original version. He had created his own version and the children
around him laughed. "Say it again," requested Arianna. As Marcelo repeated the rhyme, the children watched him just as they watch Olive.
Marcelo seemed to enjoy this and he proudly stood up. When Marcelo
was done, Arianna declared, "My turn." Several other children joined us,
and it turned into an "open mike" for spontaneous story rhymes.

Story Rhyme 1 by Marcelo

I'm a mean old witch with my mirror and then I ride my broom
with my pointy claws. My picture is bent and my picture fell on
the floor. You better watch out or I'll kick you!

Story Rhyme 2 by Isabella

I'm a mean old witch with my cat. My picture fell on the floor
and now it's ripped. And my picture got bended. My mommy
throwed it in the trash and I got sad. You better watch out or I'll
kick you!

Story Rhyme 3 by Arianna

I'm a mean old witch with my pointy hat. I ride my broom with
my pap. My shoes are pointy. My nose is too. You better watch
out or I'll chop you!

The children transformed a basic rhyming storyline into their own story
rhymes by adding new language and new action/content. The children's
rhymes (listed above in chronological order as spoken by the children)
show how closely the children listen to one another. Isabella piggybacks
on Marcelo's original idea of a "picture" and ends her rhyme with a "kick."
Arianna retains most of the original version of "I'm a Mean Old Witch"
except for changing "cat" to "pap" and ending with "chop."

As I wrote down these rhymes, 3-year-old Rima sat next to me. She
had a clipboard from our writing center and was also observing and taking notes just like me. Rima had heard Arianna's rhyme and wanted to
ask her a question. Rima took "notes" as she and the children talked:

Rima: What's a pap?
Arianna: I just said that for fun. I'm making a joke.
Isabella: What is chop?
Arianna: Chop someone up with a knife.
Marcelo: That means cut somebody.

Thanks to Rima's prompting, Arianna explained to her peers why she had specifically chosen the word *pap*. Arianna was able to explain her word choice and, in doing so, she continued the children's reflective and interactive conversation on their rhymes. Emma, a 4-year-old English language learner, then came over and shared a rhyme:

Story Rhyme 4 by Emma

If I'm pointing my shoes I cut somebody with my knife.

Emma's rhyme shows that she paid close attention to the children's conversation and incorporated certain words (*knife, pointing, shoes*) in her rhyme. Rima then contributed the last rhyme:

Story Rhyme 5 by Rima

I'm a mean old witch with a pointy hat and shoes too. You better watch out or I'll take your shoe.

Being both creative and confident in her language skills, Rima did not need the ideas of her peers and created her own version based on Olive's original.

When the children finished their rhymes, they wanted to see my notes. The children were proud of their rhymes and wanted to bring them home. After I made a photocopy of their story rhymes, Isabella went to the writing center and began to draw on her paper. Arianna followed and said, "I'm going to draw a picture of the witch." Isabella replied, "I'm writing down my rhyme." From Olive's original telling of the rhyme, the children then extended it to their own creative story rhymes told to one another, and then finally to written representations of their rhymes. The children's retellings and reformulations both in oral language, and also in drawing and writing, serve as additional child-initiated steps toward gaining a stronger sense of story. Since Olive's rhymes are shorter and easier to remember than her longer stories, the children use them as a framework or springboard for creating their own.

THE ROLE OF THE AUDIENCE

During Olive's storytelling sessions, the children demonstrated their ability to listen and play important roles in the storytelling process. The stories that called for the children's participation were the most popular among the children. The children also loved stories that incorporated rhyme, repetitive phrases, body movements, and unique words (Isbell, 2002). Olive's telling of "The Screeching Door," a story based on *The Squeaking Door* as retold by MacDonald (2006), included many of these elements. Olive explained that this story came to her over 20 years ago "in true oral tradition fashion— from one storyteller to another." The story was unfamiliar to my group of children and I was surprised to see 3-year-old Isabella's ability to remember the story's numerous characters (Sarah, Grandma, cat, dog, snake, goat, and donkey) and the gestures to represent each character.

At the beginning of the story, Sarah, a young girl, is accompanied by only a cat as she tries to fall asleep one night at her grandmother's house. As the story progresses, one animal is added to each refrain until there is a long list of companions to remember as well as the accompanying verbal and physical responses. For the snake, Olive and the children quietly hiss "ssssssss" as they put their hands together and move them in the shape of an "s" to signify slithering. The language and structure of the story invite the children to imitate Olive and join in the storytelling experience.

As Olive and the children told the story, some children turned to peers or teachers as if to confirm the story's events. They exchanged glances when finding something satisfying, funny, sad, or scary. Some children responded with hugs, handholding, pats on the back, and nudges. Three-year-old Isabella physically responded to the story in varied ways (see Figure 4.2).

In between keeping up with copying Olive's physical and verbal responses, Isabella managed to pause twice to look over at me (see the fifth and eighth frames). Isabella looked at me when Olive snored loudly, as if to say, "Nadia, isn't Olive silly?" I smiled to show that I agreed with her. After my response, Isabella continued to engage with the story, and giggled with the children as she joined them in pretending to be a goat (see the 10th frame).

MY PERSONAL STORIES—
THE VALUE FOR ADULT-CHILD BONDS
AND LANGUAGE LEARNING

Inspired by Olive, I found myself becoming a storyteller through telling personal stories about small things that I did.

"Nadia, Did Anyone Laugh at You Today?"

As I walked to my car last night, I noticed a huge branch lying on the side of the road next to a tree. I thought to myself, "I could use this branch in my classroom." I was not sure how we could use it, but I knew we would

Figure 4.2. Isabella Participates in *The Squeaking Door*

think of something. Before picking up the branch, I looked around to see if anyone was around. If someone saw me, they might think I was silly for walking around at night with a huge stick. The coast was clear, so I picked up the stick and brought it to school the next day.

I told this story to the children after Marcelo asked, "Nadia, where did you get that branch?" At the moment, I did not realize that my explanation would draw a gathering of children around me. As I told the children about my experience finding the branch, I remember using a lively voice to engage them and I could feel all eyes on me. The children thought my story of how I found the branch was funny. They giggled and asked me what we would do with the branch.

Later that day, as I helped Marcelo put his nap blanket away, he said, "Nadia, did anyone laugh at you today?"

"Marcelo," I said, "I am not sure what you are asking me about. Can you tell me more?"

"Like when you found the stick," Marcelo said. "Nobody laughed at you?"

I realized that Marcelo was referring to a line in my branch story.

"If someone saw me, they might think I was silly for walking around at night with a huge branch."

He seemed concerned about me and wanted to make sure that I felt safe. I hugged Marcelo and said, "Thank you for asking. Nobody laughed at me today."

Like most of Olive's stories, my story about the stick seemed to have a moral: It is not nice to laugh at others.

Reflecting on this experience, I realized that without thinking about or planning it, I myself had become a storyteller in some of my interactions with the children. The branch story re-ignited my awareness and interest in the value of personal stories for connecting with the children as well as in promoting language skills. Children show genuine interest and are intrigued with personal narratives of adults and children, and ask deep questions that show thought and attention. Marcelo took a keen interest in my story and showed concern for me. The story brought us closer together in an emotional connection.

"Will You Tell Me the Bee Story?

One day, as I set out new materials for our nature center, I noticed that a few children were gathering around me to watch. I showed them the insects in my box and the books I had selected for us. We organized these materials in baskets and added magnifying glasses as a finishing touch. As I walked toward my desk to put the box away, I noticed that a few children stayed to explore the materials.

Arianna approached me and asked, "Nadia, will you tell me the bee story?"

I paused and thought about her request. I did not know what she was referring to. "What bee story would you like me to tell you?"

Arianna responded, "The one about the bee that stung you on your hand."

It took me a moment, but I recalled the "story" Arianna referred to and I sat down with her to tell it. The children at the nature center joined us and they giggled as I retold the tale of my bee sting.

Two months earlier, I had explained to Arianna why I had a big bandage on my hand. Until the day 2 months later when Arianna requested an encore, I had not considered it "a story." But as I retold it to the group of children, I remembered the techniques I had learned from Olive and was conscious of my body language and tone of voice. When I re-enacted getting stung by the bee, I yelled "Ouch!" and the children leaned on each other and laughed. My story also seemed to teach a lesson: If a bee stings you, you will be all right—a reassuring moral for all children.

Arianna also reminded me of another detail: "Tell us how you were holding your baby."

I was surprised that Arianna had also remembered this detail in my story. Arianna's interest in my personal bee story seemed to be a link to learning about me and the world outside school. As in my interaction with Marcelo and my branch story, I felt as though my story had brought Arianna and me closer together, though very much through Arianna's initiative and not mine.

I have found that using personal stories in the classroom benefits children by:

- Personalizing teaching
- Strengthening adult-child bonds
- Helping form a sense of community
- Providing a language model for children to imitate
- Inspiring children to tell their own stories
- Acknowledging individual and cultural linguistic identity
- Contributing to a language-rich environment

As I told these personal stories, something I had never done before Olive's work in our room, I felt I was really learning the art of storytelling. As the teller, I put the techniques I had observed and learned into practice and gained a better understanding of Olive's role in the classroom. I especially relied on making eye contact with the children—as I told a story, I looked at the children, and in return, the children looked at me. This helped the children stay connected to my story and I also enjoyed seeing their facial expressions. Eye contact contributed to making storytelling a personal experience, and it transferred to our other interactions during the day.

From Olive, I learned the art of oral storytelling and the role of storyteller for building community and fostering new and meaningful language experiences for young children. By observing closely, I witnessed first-hand the influence of telling a story and the excitement and the sense of community it creates for children and teachers. Olive's stories and rhymes inspired my own storytelling, as well as the children's, and I developed my own storytelling traditions and rituals. I now see that personal stories are just as powerful as learned tales shared orally. As a teacher, I now see multiple ways that stories incorporate language into the curriculum. The inclusion of storytelling in the classroom serves as a tool to support children's verbal communication skills, story comprehension, and oral retelling. From Olive's stories and my own, the children used these stories as stepping-stones for creating their own stories and exploring their imaginations and understanding of the world.

REFERENCES

Barton, B., & Booth, D. (1990). *Stories in the classroom: Storytelling, reading aloud and roleplaying with children*. Markham, Ontario: Pembroke Publishers Limited.

Chase, R. (1948). *Grandfather tales*. Boston: Houghton Mifflin Company.

Cooper, L. (Ha-yen-doh-nees). (1995). *Seneca Indian stories*. New York: The Greenfield Review Press.

Cooper, P. (1993). *When stories come to school: Telling, writing and performing stories in the early childhood classroom*. New York: Teachers and Writers Collaborative.

Ferlatte, D. (1997). *Knick knack paddy whack: Mother goose on the loose and other tiny tales*. Oakland, CA: Diane Ferlatte.

Isbell, R. (2002). Telling and retelling stories: Learning language and literacy. *Young Children*, 57(2), 26–30.

MacDonald, M. (2006). *The squeaking door*. New York: Harper Collins Publishers.

Paley, V. G. (1981). *Wally's stories*. Cambridge, MA: Harvard University Press.

Stadler, M. A., & Ward, G. C. (2005). Supporting the narrative development of young children. *Early Childhood Education Journal*, 33(2), 73–80.

PART II

STORIES
and
CHILDREN'S
MULTILINGUAL
LEARNING

Chapter 5

How Social Stories Support the Early Literacy Learning of Toddlers

KIM HUGHES

Kim Hughes owns and operates a family childcare in her home, and is interested in the role of stories in facilitating social learning and language growth in her young toddlers. Kim has been a family childcare provider since 1984, is a mentor to new family childcare providers, and is a part-time instructor in the Department of Elementary Education at San Francisco State University. Kim received both her B.A and M.A. from San Francisco State University.

INTRODUCTION

Nick, 28 months old, had his first day In childcare today. He was very reluctant to cross the threshold and actually come into the playroom. "Come on in, Nick, we're playing with trainsl" I tempted him. Nick and his mama slowly came into the playroom and I photographed the two of them. Nick's mother stayed for several minutes and then gave him a big hug and reminded him that she would be back soon. With a little bit of encouragement, Nick gradually joined Arturo and Zack at the train tracks. I snapped another quick picture. Not long after, the trains ceased being much of a distraction, and Nick began crying in earnest. I picked him up, and after a few minutes of cuddling and quiet reminders that his "mama would be back soon," he relaxed. My co-teacher snapped a picture of Nick smiling in my arms just before he rejoined his new friends in the playroom. Ninety minutes later, Nick's mama returned, and a quick picture documented the fact that he had survived his first day in childcare! Thanks to the miracle of instant print, the four pictures I took on Nick's first day became part of a "social story" to help Nick and his parents visually reenact a new and somewhat scary experience for all of them.

I OPERATE A small family childcare program in my home. My program uses a "primary caregiver" model that teams one teacher with three children. The children in the program attend 2 or 3 days per week, so I have a total of six children for whom I provide primary care during the week, although we have a total of 12 children enrolled. All of the children in the program are between 19 and 29 months at the start of each school year.

The most difficult part of our school year is often the first few weeks, when children transition into what is usually their first experience with out-of-home care. Because I am always looking for new strategies to make the transitional experience as non-stressful as possible, I was fascinated to read about how one toddler program used something called a "social story" to ease one child's entrance into a new childcare center (Briody & McGarry, 2005). I was further intrigued to read that social stories are used almost exclusively with autistic children to help them "rehearse" stressful situations in advance. I decided to implement social stories to help my children's emotional transition to school. As I did so, I also discovered that the social stories promoted positive language and literacy experiences for new language learners.

CONSTRUCTING SOCIAL STORIES

Social stories are simple, usually no more than a few pages long, and help guide children through simple tasks such as how to greet a new acquaintance or what to expect from a trip to the grocery store. I wanted to create a short book, with photographs and simple text to help the children in my care understand that I was there to be their primary caregiver, that they could enjoy their time in childcare, and most important, that their parent would be back at the end of the day.

To create a social story for each child, we took photographs of the child, parent, and primary caregiver on the child's first day. We printed the photos that evening, and on each child's second day, we presented the child with a "social story book" consisting of:

1. A picture of the parent and child entering the classroom and being welcomed by the child's primary caregiver
2. A picture of the child engaged with a toy, activity, or another child
3. A picture of the child engaging at some level with his primary caregiver
4. A picture of the parent and child reuniting at the end of the short visit

We also attached direct text to each photo, such as "Mommy and [child] come to school," "[Child] has fun at school," "[Teacher] takes good care of [child]," and "At the end of the day, Mommy [or Daddy] comes back!" We made two copies of each book with a simple classroom laminating machine and a book-binding machine. One copy stayed at school, while the other went home with the child. We asked parents to make the social story available to the child at home, and to change the language of the text to fit the family setting, such as changing "Daddy" to "Papi" or translating the story into the child's home language. We asked parents to read the story with the child at least once a day for the first week of care, and then to read it anytime the child requested it. At school, the stories were kept in a basket on a low shelf and were available to children at any time.

SOCIAL STORIES AS
SOCIAL SUPPORT FOR LANGUAGE LEARNING

In very young children with limited language skills, it is often difficult to allow them to "tell their own stories" (Dalli, 2000). I found that social stories helped my very young children communicate more effectively than they might otherwise. I also found that careful observation and attention to children's voice and intonation revealed more insightful interpretations of children's thoughts and intentions.

Promoting Conversation

The following transcript was recorded approximately 2 weeks after Nick (age 28 months) and Arturo (age 19 months) started care. Nick spoke only English, while Arturo spoke Spanish and very limited English and the three teachers in the program spoke with Arturo in Spanish. One day, Nick and Arturo were the only children in the playroom and were engaged in parallel play. After 30 minutes, though, Nick picked up the basket that holds all of the children's social stories and hunted for his. In the process, the basket tipped over and all of the social stories spilled onto the carpet, arousing Arturo's attention, and he quickly moved over near Nick.

> *Arturo:* (Picks up one of the social stories, although not his own.)
>   *Mi, Mi!* [me or mine]
> *Nick:* (anxiously sorting through the stories) Oh, no, where are
>   my mamas? Where is you at? [referring to me]
> *Arturo:* (Looks at Nick, repeats "oh no" but without much
>   emphasis. Finds his own social story.) Mi!(He slowly starts to

page through his book, from front to back. He pauses at the photo showing him with his mother.) Mami! (At the page where the photo shows me holding him, he turns to me.) Mi.

Kim: Do you see Arturo?

Arturo: Mi! (as he points to me in the photo)

Kim: Sí, allí Kim. [Yes, there is Kim.]

Nick: (Having found his social story, Nick turns to the picture of his mama holding him.) I love my mama! (He points to the text.)

Kim: Yes, you love your mama!

Nick: And mommy too! [Nick has two mothers, although only one appears in the photos in the social story book.]

Nick: And Kim takes good care of me! (He turns to the photo in his book that depicts me holding him.)

Kim: Yes, I do!

Nick: And you Kim!

Kim: I am Kim, I agree.

Nick: YOU take care of ME!

Kim: Yes, I take good care of you.

Nick: (Picks up each social story in turn, opens it to the page of me holding each child.) Kim takes good care of Marti!

Kim: Yes, I do. (We repeat this ritual with all six social stories in the basket. Arturo looks on intently, and clutches his own story to his chest.) *Mi!* [mine]

Nick has clearly memorized the text of his social story. The language he used is word-for-word from the actual text. Although Nick spoke very clearly and quite proficiently for his age (28 months), he often mixed up his syntax. Without the prior rehearsal of reading the story over and over, both at school and at home, I would have expected him to say something more like "Marti, you take good care!" The fact that he knew exactly what the text said indicates that he had heard the book far more often than I had read it to him at childcare. I had only read it to him two or three times. Although he enjoyed looking at the photos in his story, and often brought the book to me to look at with him, he was much more interested in flipping to a particular photo than going page by page through the book and listening to the text.

The emphasis that Nick put on his connection with me, his primary caregiver, suggests that he clearly understood that he had a relationship with me that differed from his relationships with the other teachers. The tone of voice he used as he announced, "*You* take care of *me*!" indicates ownership and attachment that I generally hear when he shouts, "But that's mine!" Briody and McGarry (2005) discuss how using a social story to help a typically developing 2-year-old acclimate to childcare also facilitated the attachment between the child and his primary caregiver: "The shared social experience [of his primary caregiver reading his social story to him at childcare] led to further opportunities for dialogue and caregiver reassurances" (p. 39).

A conversation with Erin, Nick's mother, at the end of the day confirmed that he often brought her the second copy of his social story, kept at home, to be read to him after they returned home from childcare. Erin noted that Nick spends a long time examining each photo, and she has the chance to read the accompanying text several times before he is ready to turn the page. She also usually tracks the text with her finger as she reads it, which she knows is an important early literacy skill. She also mentioned that on the days that Nick attends childcare, he is often anxious, particularly on the way in the car. To comfort him, she says, "You know, Kim is going to take good care of you today." Nick relaxes at hearing this statement, and she often extends Nick's social story by reminding him that "at the end of the day, Mama comes back!" She said that Nick likes to answer, "That's right, mama, you come back!"

Nick's mother considered Nick's social story an important rehearsal for Nick during the stressful acclimation period to childcare, and encouraged Nick to "practice" his school day in the safety and comfort of his home and car. Looking at his social story with his mother at home provides a routine for Nick to review his childcare day, which reduces his anxiety regarding the new experience. In effect, social stories promote a home-school bridge and help parents talk with their children about separation and reunion.

Support for New Language Learners

Social stories dictated in a child's home language provide a culturally relevant springboard for new language learners. Social stories in a child's first language also validate children's home lives and promote first language growth. The ease with which social stories can be translated by families into a child's home language suggests that they can be used as a teaching tool that may extend well beyond the transitional period into a childcare or preschool setting.

Several weeks into Arturo's enrollment, I had the opportunity to scaffold his English learning while we looked at his social story. Although I generally spoke to Arturo in Spanish, in an effort to support his English language acquisition, I alternated between English and Spanish as we looked at the photos.

Kim: (pointing to first picture in the social story book) *Arturo viene
a la casa de Kim.* [Arturo comes to Kim's house.] *¿Quíen es?*
[Who's that?] (pointing to a photo of Arturo's mother)
Arturo: Mama!
Kim: (at the next page, I point to a photo of Arturo playing with
trains alongside another child) *¿Quíen es?*
Arturo: Gegie [Gregory] . . . and train!
Kim: Yes, you and Gregory are playing with Thomas-the-trains!
(I turn to the next photo in the social story, which shows me
holding a smiling Arturo in my arms) *Y, ¿Quíen es?*
Arturo: Kim! (I turn to the last page in the book, the page that is
generally everyone's favorite, because it contains a photo of
mommy embracing her child at the end of the day. Before I
can ask, "*¿Quíen es?*" Arturo shouts.) Mama come back!

I knew that Arturo had heard his social story read to him verbatim
on numerous occasions, and I wanted to extend his language learning
by asking questions. When I asked "*¿Quíen es?*" Arturo surprised me
by replying in English, "Mama come back!" Our shared activity became
a multilingual experience that demonstrated Arturo's emerging English
comprehension. Arturo had heard social stories read in English to other
children, and correctly identified "Mama comes back!" as the text that
accompanies the photo of a parent reuniting with her child.

Social stories can be texts in a child's home language that validate the
child's first language, and multilingual texts that promote oral and written
language development in more than one language. Although Arturo had
only heard his own social story read to him in Spanish, both at home and
at school, he had heard other children's stories read to them in English.
While I can only speculate that he recognized that they were the same
stories in either language, there is a distinct possibility that this connection will become more powerful as his multilingual skills increase. When
children overhear social stories read to other children in a language other
than their first language, it supports new language learning as children
are exposed to new vocabulary, syntax, and phonology.

Tabors (2008) discusses the concept of "spectating," which refers to
"active observations by the second-language-learning children when they
are in close proximity to English speakers and are focusing on the language that is being used" (p. 51). Tabors notes that this behavior occurs
when children interact or play side by side. When Arturo was very aware
that both he and Nick, a slightly older playmate, were focusing on their
social stories, Arturo used this experience with a more accomplished English speaker to scaffold his own new language learning in English. Tabors

(2008) also notes that another type of language learning occurs in social situations, "rehearsing," which refers to second language learners "practicing" certain words or phrases without actually understanding what the words mean or intending to use them to communicate. In Nick and Arturo's interaction, Arturo repeated what he has just heard Nick say ("oh no"), but he did not yet understand the relevance of the words and so was rehearsing what he had heard.

LEARNING FROM SOCIAL STORIES

As an early childhood educator, it was enormously inspiring for me to read how one teacher used social stories to help a toddler transition into a childcare center. By trying to replicate this success in my own small family childcare center, I found that social stories helped children during the difficult acclimation process by allowing them to sort out their feelings with simple dialogue and photos. Given this first level of support, the social stories also enriched the children's multilingual oral and written language experiences. The fact that the social stories are *books* glaringly made them integral early literacy resources, and they have become part of the print-rich environment that I know aids children in their love of reading and literature in more than one language.

Giving parents copies of the books and asking them to make them available to their children at home promoted a sense of trust and comfort for the children, and encouraged cross-language use between home and school. Recently, a young boy who spoke Hebrew started in my program. With his mother's help, we constructed his social story using Hebrew letters, and arranged the book so that it was read from right to left as is correct in Hebrew. Eyal, only 22 months old, could not read, but as he thumbed through his social story he carefully traced the letters with his finger, and always turned the pages from right to left. When it is Eyal's turn to choose a book for us to read during circle time, he always picked his social story. He always presented the book to us so that we could turn the pages from right to left. We read his story in English, and he occasionally repeated a word or phrase that he heard, particularly "come back." His mother laughingly told me that he insisted on "reading" his book to his baby brother every night. He usually "read" the book in Hebrew, but his mother reported that he just recently he said, "*Ima* [mother] come back!" Eyal is usually silent while he is in our care, but hearing his social story read to him in English at school and in Hebrew at home allowed him to begin to connect the two languages. Although none of the teachers in my program speaks Hebrew, writing Eyal's social story in Hebrew provided him with a link to his family that we could not have duplicated in English alone.

The ease with which the books can be translated and dictated into a child's home language is clearly a key component of providing culturally relevant language experiences for children. At the same time, while the new language learners in my program benefited from hearing their stories read in their home language, they also heard other children's social stories read to them in English, providing a support for additional language acquisition as well. All the children in my program benefited from hearing the stories read to each child in several languages—it promoted a knowledge of cultural and linguistic diversity that would be hard to duplicate with traditional children's books alone.

Using social stories in my family childcare program not only contributed to the language and literacy development of the children in my care, but demonstrated that even veteran teachers like myself can add new tricks to our teaching repertoire. Social stories have expanded my own knowledge of how stories can support children's social development and multilingualism, and I look forward to using them in various ways in the years to come.

REFERENCES

Briody, J., & McGarry, K. (2005). Using social stories to ease children's transitions. *Young Children, 60*(5), 38–42.

Dalli, C. (2000). Starting childcare: What young children learn about relating to adults in the first weeks of starting childcare. *Early childhood research and practice, 2.* Retrieved August 5, 2006 from http://ecrp.uiuc.edu/v2n2/dalli.html

Tabors, P. O. (2008). *One child, two languages: A guide for early childhood educators of children learning English as a second language* (2nd ed.). Baltimore: Paul H. Brooks.

Chapter 6

Pictures in Our Lives: Using Wordless Picture Books with New Language Learners

NATHAN WEBER

Nathan Weber has an M.A. from San Francisco State University and is a pre-school teacher in San Francisco. His interests include how issues of race, class, and gender intersect with preschool curriculum. He is also interested in first and second language acquisition, teacher inquiry groups, teachers as mentors, and therapeutic preschools.

I BOUGHT SEVERAL wordless picture books (books with little or no text) at a library book sale, including *Truck* (1980) by Donald Crews, *Window* (1991) by Jeannie Baker, and *The Winner* (1969) by Kjell Ringi. I decided to put them in the book area to see if my preschoolers showed any interest. Little did I expect that this would be the beginning of a new reading experience for both me and my English learners. After I introduced the wordless books to our classroom, I saw children who rarely chose to "read" books carrying the wordless picture books to other areas of the classroom and using them to support their play. The children's engagement with these books helped me think about how the images of stories support new language learners. I also noticed how I "read" story books with children, how children see themselves as readers, and how pictures offer rich language learning opportunities. I saw the benefits of valuing pictures equally with words, found a new way to see my children as active meaning makers, and reflected on the importance of pictures in our lives.

In this chapter, I take an inquiry stance that aims to notice children's strengths and preferences and improve my practice with young children learning English through wordless picture books. Wordless picture books differ from other types of literature and visual art because the pictures are intended to assist in telling stories (Nodelman, 1988). Nodelman's research details how children's picture books are a valuable and unique literary genre, and examines topics such as using style to convey meaning, the contextual meaning of visual objects, and children as viewers and interpreters of pictures. Wordless picture books also promote book handling behaviors, connect reading with our visually dominated culture, support children's special needs, and inspire multiple forms of storytelling (Jalongo, Dragich, Conrad, & Zhang, 2002).

These flexible aspects of wordless picture books promote meaningful personal relationships between children and books. And as Lysaker (2006) noticed, "If we are constituted by, through and within meaning-making events, then a curriculum rich with opportunities for authentic encounters with literacy and with others in purposeful, meaningful work is essential" (p. 21). Because wordless picture books require telling a story by looking at a sequence of pictures, rather than reading words, they can support children's voices at various levels of English learning. I want to validate children's ways of reading and thinking while still being able to encourage further learning. The children presented—Kevin, Ashley, and Brent—are composite portraits of my 4 years of experiences working with new language learners in urban preschools around three texts: *Truck, Window,* and *The Winner.*

(RE)READING *TRUCK*—SEEING KEVIN AS A READER

Kevin is a 3-year-old English learner in his first year of school. Kevin tends to shy away from strangers by hiding behind a familiar adult or tilting his head down and looking at the floor. He often plays alone, and when he speaks, it is with a soft voice. His play preferences for 2 months in the middle of the year were the cars and trucks in the block area, which usually puts him at one end of the classroom, away from the books. Every morning Kevin's mom reads him one book in English before she leaves, usually *Brown Bear, Brown Bear* (1992) or *Polar Bear, Polar Bear* (1991), both by Bill Martin Jr. and Eric Carle. Kevin seems to enjoy this, smiling, laughing, and allowing other children to sit with him. After his mom leaves, he might choose to follow a teacher, use the play dough, or play with cars and trucks.

One day, as I hoped, Kevin noticed *Truck* on the shelf and shouted excitedly, "Truck!" Kevin pointed to the red truck on the cover. He reached for it and pulled it into his lap as he slipped onto the couch. He waved me over and I sat next to him as he opened to the first page, and then to the next. He finally stopped on the third page, where a great big red truck took up both pages of the book. "Truck!" Kevin said excitedly, his finger pressed onto the pages. "That's right. It's a truck." I pointed at the white lettering and moved my finger left to right. Kevin zipped through the rest of the book, stopping briefly on each page to point out the red truck and shout "Truck!"

Truck tells a story of a large red truck carrying cargo from coast to coast. Signs, shapes, tunnels, exhaust smoke, and arrows are used to emphasize typical happenings along American roads and highways. Crews, reflecting on what he wants readers to take away from his books, said,

> Initially, what you want them to take away is an enjoyment of the involvement of being in books; I wasn't really thinking in terms of education or messages, or things that they needed to take away, especially. I just think of an adventure, an involvement with observation, a learning to look, to be more observant about what you see. (Bodmer, 1998, p. 6)

Kevin and I read the book 10 times that day, and in the afternoon he sat alone reading the book. I did not expect he would be so enthusiastic about Truck, which showed me the power of children's preferences and how choosing story books hinges on how well we understand and know each child. My first experience reading Truck with Kevin was a new, exciting moment that left me wondering how else to read Truck with him. Reflecting on how quickly he flipped through the book, I thought he might benefit from spending more time looking at each page in Truck and naming other objects in English since he already mastered the word truck. The next day I tried to slow Kevin down by resting my hand on the page so he couldn't turn it so fast, and giving us time to point out other images on the page besides the truck.

I succeeded in slowing him down, even to the point where we became frustrated with one another. He would try to move my hand as I kept trying to redirect him. In the middle of the book there is a double-page picture resembling the busy freeways of Los Angeles, and the red truck travels with other cars and trucks on intersecting roadways. I took this as an opportunity to talk about colors. After Kevin pointed to the red truck, I started pointing at other vehicles and saying, "yellow truck," "green truck," and "blue car." He repeated some of my words, but remained occupied with trying to turn the page as I continued on with my color naming and firmly holding down the page. I wanted to use colors to talk about the other trucks in the book by building off one of the 30 English words Kevin already knew: truck. What I realized was that Kevin was reading *for* the truck. It was the reason he picked the book in the first place and it was, after all, the main topic—the very storyline—of the book. He seemed excited about being in control of the story.

In my rush to seize what I thought was a teachable moment, I questioned my assumptions about how to read stories and support new language learners. I asked myself, "Is it wrong for Kevin to flip quickly through the book and is it good or bad for second language learning? Maybe he is losing himself in the visual story, imagining how fast trucks go and replicating this speed through his page turning." I also saw the fun and challenge for Kevin in finding the truck on each page, as children love to find Waldo in *Where's Waldo?* (1997) by Martin Handford and objects in *I Spy: A Book of Picture Riddles* (1992) by Jean Marzollo. So I questioned why I wanted to emphasize oral English language development, particularly vocabulary building, with a child who seldom showed this much enthusiasm for books. I decided to back off, and continue to support Kevin's interest in wordless books by following his lead and valuing his choices. I let him first immerse himself in the story and then waited a little bit before adding more layers of English learning.

Truck remained in our classroom for 2 months, over which time Kevin took the book home twice for the weekend. Eventually, we talked about how the truck's cargo of bikes looked similar to the ones we ride in the yard. He knew the difference between "this way" and "that way," and we noticed the smoke coming from the exhaust pipes. I learned to become less concerned with learning new vocabulary or high-frequency words, and instead to talk more informally, such as "I like this car" or "I want to look at that page again." I felt like we were working and learning together, as both he and I slowed our pace. I looked forward to our conversations over this now familiar text, reading it again and again, each time seemingly similar, yet different. Kevin showed me the power of one text to empower a young language learner, both as a reader of books and as a speaker. Kevin also gained self-esteem from seeing himself as a reader and eventually felt comfortable saying new words; also, our bond over reading extended into other activities in the classroom such as circle time, cooking, and art.

SPENDING TIME AT THE WINDOW: ASHLEY'S QUESTIONS

On the front cover of my copy of Jeannie Baker's *Window* (1991) is a quote from *Booklist:* "A good way of introducing environmental concerns to the young." I saw the commentary on urban growth in the book, but I was unsure whether the environmental concerns would be a good story emphasis for young language learners. I thought my children would be drawn to the book's beautifully crafted relief collage art from materials that Baker collected. *Window* explores "the concept of exponential change" where a mother and baby look out a window at the wilderness (http://www.jeanniebaker.com). As Sam the baby grows, the view changes from house, to village, to city until the young man marries and moves to the country with his child. I was curious about how my children would interpret this book.

The first child to take *Window* from the shelf and ask me to read it was 3½-year-old Ashley, a native Mandarin speaker. She is comfortable trying her English in the classroom and often speaks English to the Mandarin-speaking teachers, although she speaks Mandarin more than half the time. She prefers dramatic play over books, and loves to role-play cats and dogs, mommies and babies, and cashier at a grocery store. At times, she uses Mandarin to make a joke or have me say baby words. Recently, Ashley has been pushing books out of my hand when I am reading with other children, but is not interested in joining the reading group. She wants me to stop reading and follow her to another area, sometimes pulling my arm as I say, "I am reading right now, but will come with you when I am done." When Ashley asked me to read *Window*, I did not know what to expect. I said, "Let's look at the pictures because there are no words."

Once in the book area, Ashley sat in my lap and opened the book as I read the title. She repeated, "Window." Her hand flat on the page, she turned to the dedication page, then to the first page with a picture. She quickly pointed out, "Baby, cat, bird!" As she turned the pages, she renamed the baby "a boy" on page three and named animals in the beginning, but started to notice the many cars later in the book. She also pointed out the cat in every scene, sometimes spending a few extra minutes to search. I noticed I was repeating words she used and sometimes adding action to the images she was labeling. For example, "It's a boy. Is he going to school?" I wanted to give Ashley an open-ended reading experience where I was building off her interests and her vocabulary rather than telling a story.

Ashley was drawn to images relevant to her experiences and interests, so instead of seeing the environment changing from nature to city, she read the story of the baby and cat introduced on the first page. She noticed how the baby was growing up, like her. Unlike my reading with Kevin, Ashley and I spent 3 to 5 minutes looking closely at each picture, pointing out familiar images that she spontaneously labeled in English. Toward the end, she asked for words to identify images she did not know, such as *rocket, kite,* and *suitcase.* Ashley never saw the urban development as the main storyline, although it surely was the intention of the author.

Instead, she created her own story out of her experience as a developing child.

Ashley related her life to the pictures in the book, noticing familiar objects that allowed her to use her developing English and asking me for new vocabulary. The book became a springboard for a conversation about turning 4 and how being older is important to Ashley. We talked about the concept of growing up through Ashley's past, being a baby, and her future, turning 4 soon. I was intrigued by Ashley's ability to relate to the story and how she seemed to understand the concept of something happening over time, such as growing older or the phenomenon of urban sprawl. Because *Window* places the viewer inside the picture—the viewer is inside a room looking out a window at the world—children are able to be first-person narrators. Ashley put herself in the context of the room, looking out the window, which allowed the personal to work itself into her reading of the book.

Later that same day, I saw Ashley on the couch in the reading area introducing the book to one of her peers. She pointed out the cat in English to Mandy, who speaks Cantonese, and Mandy followed her example by repeating, "Cat." I noticed them pointing at different objects and saying, "It's mine," or "I have it." When they finished reading, they went to play with baby dolls and kitchen props in the house area. Reading *Window* with Ashley developed her storytelling skills, new vocabulary, and confidence in being a young reader. I was excited that Ashley was sharing a familiar text with another child who was learning English, too. Ashley, confident that she was a reader, used her recent experience to support another child who is learning to speak English. Even though Ashley rarely joined group reading times, she did begin to ask teachers to read individually with her. I also noticed that if she were sitting in a teacher's lap, she was more accepting of other children joining her. Toward the end of the year, I would revisit *Window* when Ashley turned 4 years old. During a gardening unit designed to bring environmental awareness into the curriculum, Ashley noticed that plants, like babies, have to grow up. She became our classroom reminder to her peers to handle the plants carefully.

I'M BIGGER THAN YOU—BRENT THE DINOSAUR

In many preschools I've heard children say, "I'm bigger than you." This simple phrase has many different meanings and interpretations. Often, it means that a child is literally taller or older than a peer. On the other hand, being bigger can be more abstract, such as how some children imagine being invincible, powerful, and important in a world that is truly bigger than them. In my experience, I notice children mastering how to use language when conveying messages of power and control to others. Being bigger, or better, means being able to compare yourself to another person, who, by definition, is smaller. Three-year-old Brent is interested in what it means to be big.

Brent stomps around the classroom with his arms tucked inside his T-shirt so they look shorter. He bares his teeth at every child who comes within 4 feet. He repeatedly informs everyone that he is a T-Rex and eats meat. He says, "We [humans] are meat." He is excellent at pretending, never once needing to touch another child to send them reeling in fear. Watching Brent crane his neck and deliberately stomp in slow motion, I'm always amazed at his accurate movements.

Brent has advanced English language skills compared with other new language learners in my classroom, and I've never heard him speak his first language of Spanish in the classroom, even to his parents. None of the teachers speaks Spanish fluently, but Brent likes to be read to by adults in English, and he keeps choosing books until a teacher needs to stop reading. I have not seen Brent read by himself, which I found surprising because he always showed interest in books in our interactions. At first, I thought that Brent's book experience centered on adults and that perhaps because he could not decode words, he did not see himself as a reader of stories. My goal was to give Brent a successful book experience without needing to read words to tell a story. One day I decided to share *The Winner* (Ringi, 1969), a wordless book about two nameless men who start off facing one another in their underwear, then one leaves and comes back with a top hat, cane, glasses, and a moustache. The other leaves and returns wearing a fancy uniform and carrying a flag. They both try to outdo each other until one eventually rides in on a big blue fire-breathing dinosaur that ends up eating them both and running off.

I introduced *The Winner* to Brent during an afternoon free play. I noticed that the children had not selected it yet, perhaps because the cover was not appealing and lacked the catchy pictures that seem to adorn many of our books. As we opened the book, Brent looked at me and waited for me to start reading. I pointed to the first page and said, "Look." I sat silently as Brent flipped the pages. The conflict in the story between the characters escalates as each character tries to one-up the other, which he found funny. At the story's end, Brent saw the pictures of the dinosaur eating both characters, and asked me, "What happened?" I suggested we read it again right then to find out. By giving prompts, I encouraged Brent to use "and then" statements to tell the story the second time. I only prompted three times before Brent used "and then" without me asking, "And then what happened?" Brent described what he saw and then

I would add something I noticed. We went back and forth a few times as the pictures grew more complex. He was able to point out what he could label, or ask for the name. I could introduce new vocabulary or notice something that might give Brent an idea. For example, noticing the character walking off the side of the page to get something reminded Brent that the pink horse is next. Also, using language for emotions adds to the layers of English learning. When the blue dinosaur appears, Brent remembers that the dinosaur eats the two characters, so I "notice" that one of the characters is scared of the dinosaur. Brent says he is scared of the fire. "But dinosaurs do not have fire," I said. On the last page, where the dinosaur appears to be running off into the white background, Brent said, "And then the dinosaur ate them. Why?"

I was glad to hear Brent using "and then" as a narrative strategy because it helped him continue telling the story while still focusing on describing what was happening in the pictures. I also noticed that Brent started using "and then" statements in conversations—for example, when he told me about his trip to the doctor the following week. But what caught my attention and is something I still reflect on was his "Why?" question at the end of the book. Brent could be asking a number of questions: Why *would* a dinosaur eat two people? Why do the two main characters get eaten? Are they bad guys and deserve to be eaten? Does one-upping each other mean we will both die? I wasn't sure what Brent was asking, but I said that the dinosaur must have been hungry. To which he replied, as he gripped the flesh on his left forearm, "Because we're meat."

CONCLUSION

Wordless picture books are complex, but not necessarily complicated. It is a mistake to think they are too simple, lesser than books with words, or hard to use in the classroom because they are wordless. Instead, they offer reading choices for children and teachers, develop ideas and language through description and interpretation of pictures, and challenge how teachers develop our approach to English learning. They offer individualized learning experiences for children, and for teachers, opportunities to develop reflective teaching practices.

Each composite child approached books and storytelling in unique ways that revealed their strengths and ways of learning. In the case of Kevin, he took control of reading *Truck*, which put me in an uncomfortable position as a teacher who usually reads to children. I needed to stop and think, "Do I validate and value Kevin's way of reading *Truck*?" The open-endedness of wordless picture books created room for Kevin to interpret the story and read without stress. I believe because Kevin was able to start where he felt comfortable by just saying, "Truck," that over the following months of revisiting the same text he used English to make comparisons, express his interests, and participate in group readings. For a young language learner, a love and understanding of books is beneficial for the development of new languages in the classroom.

Ashley was able to express her knowledge of English by labeling objects in *Window*, but also started to ask for new vocabulary. I noticed that she understood that the book illustrated something happening over time and related it to her own life. She eventually took her new experience and invited another English-learning peer to read with her, an unexpected result that benefited both children's English learning. For Brent, who is essentially bilingual, I wanted to encourage him to see himself as a reader rather than depending on adults to tell stories. Brent was able to acquire a new strategy for telling stories: "and then" statements. Brent's curiosity was apparent when he asked, "Why?" This simple question does not always have a simple answer. What does Brent mean and how are my answers understood?

Wordless picture books encourage meaningful interactions that center on children's interests, and these interactions are critical for new language learning in preschool classrooms even without all the answers. Through the use of wordless picture books I found ways to slow down and follow my children's lead, notice the different ways children think about language learning, and change how I used wordless picture books. In my experience, the more personal classrooms are for children, the more responsive they become to learning. Why else do children learn the first letter of their name so quickly, or of their friends? Here I return to the individualization of curriculum by thinking about the placement of the child (viewer) to the text (curriculum) and how learning seems to emerge from the child when personal stories are valued.

Wordless picture books allow multiple ways to tell stories, which often vary based on ethnicity or cultural background (Wang & Leichtman, 2000; Curenton & Justice, 2004), but also on the individual child. Wordless picture books offer opportunities for young English language learners to create positive, individualized, and child-centered experiences with books that lead to seeing themselves as competent readers and storytellers. They also offer teachers, like myself, the opportunity to question teaching expectations and strategies in promoting story book "reading" with young children.

REFERENCES

Baker, J. (1991). *Window*. New York: Puffin Books.

Bodmer, G. (1998). Donald Crews: The signs and times of an American childhood—essay and interview. *African American Review, 32*. Retrieved January 27, 2008, from http://findarticles.com/p/articles/mi_m2838/is_n1_v32/ai_20610477

Crews, D. (1980). *Truck*. New York: Greenwillow Books.

Curenton, S. M., & Justice, L. M. (2004). African American and Caucasian preschoolers' use of decontextualized language: Literate language features in oral narratives. *Language, Speech, and Hearing Services in Schools, 35,* 240–253.

Handford, M. (1997). *Where's Waldo?* Cambridge, MA: Candlewick Press.

Jalongo, M. R., Dragich, D., Conrad, N. K., & Zhang, A. (2002). Using wordless picture books to support emergent literacy. *Early Childhood Education Journal, 29*(3), 167–177.

Lysaker, J. T. (2006). Young children's readings of wordless picture books: What's 'self' got to do with it? *Journal of Early Childhood Literacy, 6*(1), 33–55.

Martin Jr., B., & Carle, E. (1991). *Polar bear, polar bear, what do you hear?* New York: Henry Holt and Company.

Martin Jr., B., & Carle, E. (1992). *Brown bear, brown bear, what do you see?* New York: Henry Holt and Company.

Marzollo, J. (1992). *I spy: A book of picture riddles*. New York: Scholastic.

Nodelman, P. (1988). *Words about pictures: The narrative art of children's picture books*. Athens, GA: University of Georgia Press.

Ringi, K. (1969). *The winner*. New York: Harper & Row.

Wang, Q., & Leichtman, M. D. (2000). Same beginnings, different stories: A comparison of American and Chinese children's narratives. *Child Development, 71*(5), 1329–1346.

Chapter 7

Personal Stories as a Home-School Link in a Bilingual Kindergarten

LORI OLDHAM

Lori Oldham is a Spanish bilingual elementary school teacher in the San Francisco Bay area. She taught first grade for 4 years and is currently a kindergarten teacher. Before teaching children, she taught ESL to adults for 3 years. She is interested in how first language development affects second language development in bilingual children.

OUR DAY IN my Spanish/English bilingual kindergarten began like all the rest. We chanted the alphabet, recited our high-frequency words, and completed the phonemic awareness activity from our scripted reading program. Moving from our warm-up activities into our children's literature selection, I wondered if anything from today's story about weather would peak the children's interest. We were in the middle of winter, which here in northern California means a lot of rain, so I assumed the children would have personal experiences to relate to the story. Before reading the story, I asked the children about the day's weather. They responded with a correct "sunny" and "cold." Next, I asked them to predict what kind of weather we might read about in the story. The children quickly said "sunny," "cloudy," and "rainy." A few children looked at our calendar with weather stickers to help them identify "windy," "foggy," and "snowy." With that, I began reading the story. Each page presented a different type of weather and showed the effect on people, animals, and the Earth.

We also discussed how we dress differently depending on the weather. We talked about weather-specific activities such as kite flying, swim-

81

ming outdoors, and making a snowperson. Our conversation was very organized and teacher-directed as I asked questions and they dutifully answered based on what they saw in the illustrations. But when we came to the storm page, the classroom came alive with the electricity of chitter-chatter, as if the lightning bolts on the page had jolted them out of a trance. Everyone had something to say. "Yeah, lightning!" "When we had a storm I heard the BOOM!" "Once it rained and the trees fell over and the leaves were all over." "There were no lights at my house." "Me, too!"

PERSONAL STORIES AS CULTURALLY RESPONSIVE TEACHING

The children's reactions indicated the kind of excitement in personal storytelling that I look for when we read a book. In these personal moments, children use language to relate their own stories to the text. Personal stories play an important part in the language development of kindergarten-age children, and they have a special role for the Spanish bilingual children I teach. In my bilingual classroom, I use Spanish about 80% of the time and English for 20%. My students primarily speak Spanish at home, and about 30% of my students attended preschool, with about half of these children in bilingual preschools. Both Spanish-language maintenance and exposure to English-language and literacy development are key goals in my classroom. And personal stories, which are developmentally appropriate and highly motivating, play a central role in this process.

It is difficult, though, to find time for personal stories in the tight schedule of our scripted reading program. But without personal stories, the children wouldn't make necessary connections to our language arts curriculum. Personal stories allow my students to share their individual experiences and have these highly personal moments validated as their classmates and I listen. Sharing our stories provides a foundation of emotional safety and trust that my students need if they are to take risks academically and develop both their first and second languages. For most of my students, the greatest academic risk they face each school day is learning English. They want to learn English but at the same time are scared of making a mistake and being laughed at. But once they have opened up and shared personal experiences, emotions, and values in their primary language, they feel more accepted and understood and are then ready to embrace the new world of school without fear.

I use personal story with my bilingual kindergartners as a way of incorporating culturally responsive teaching (CRT) into my instruction. Kathryn Au (2006) defines the characteristics of CRT as:

1. Acknowledging students' cultural heritage and how it affects their learning
2. Having a goal of educational success for diverse learners
3. Ensuring school success by linking home and school experiences
4. Maintaining home culture and language
5. Fostering social justice and equality in the classroom

Practicing culturally responsive teaching in my classroom through the use of story strengthens the academic success of my students from diverse backgrounds.

Culturally responsive teaching and personal story connected to the content of the literature encourage the children in my class to feel more secure and accepted at school. The students tell most of their stories for the first time in Spanish, so I encourage the use and promotion of the primary language of my students. They are also more comfortable using Spanish, so they are able to express their ideas more freely. As I listen and respond to my students' stories, I acknowledge and validate their cultural background and experiences. Through their stories I am able to learn about their experiences and find out how their cultural views of the world may differ from mine. I can then use this information to consider how their background may affect their learning and make modifications to my instruction. I also create an important link between the home and the school when I ask the parents and children to talk about personal stories related to an in-class theme. The children then share these stories with the class. These activities where lesson content is directly linked to the child's experiences at home are necessary for school success. I help my students become academically successful in their second language, English, by using their stories during English instruction as well. All of this together makes my students feel more comfortable in the school setting, which leads to their academic success in all areas of the curriculum.

Story also plays an essential role in including families to foster a strong home-school connection for the students in my classroom. Most kindergarten children are extending their social sphere beyond the family for the first time when they enter school. Children from diverse backgrounds, such as those from immigrant Latino families in my class, benefit from a strong link between the worlds of home and school. One home-school activity I use is to give homework assignments that ask parents and children to tell stories together. These assignments are related to certain themes and concepts that we discuss in class. Extending our discussion into the home gives students the opportunity to bring new ideas into the safe context of home and family before talking about them in the classroom.

This home-school link and family involvement makes the children's storytelling richer.

STORM STORIES—A HOME-SCHOOL HOMEWORK ACTIVITY

To extend our discussion of storms into the home, I created a homework page that went home that same day and was to be returned the following day. The short letter read:

Estimadas familias de salon 7,

Hemos estado leyendo libros sobre el tiempo y las tormentas. Mañana los niños compartirán historias de sus propias experiencias. Por favor platique con su hijo/a esta noche acerca de una tormenta u otro tiempo extremo que han experimentado. Después hagan un dibujo de lo que platicaron. Por favor de entregar el dibujo mañana.
Gracias,
Ms. Oldham

Dear Room 7 families,

We have been reading books about the weather and storms. Tomorrow the children will share stories of their own experiences. Please talk with your child tonight about a storm or other extreme weather event they have experienced. Afterward, draw a picture of what you discussed. Please return the drawing to class tomorrow.
Thank you,
Ms. Oldham

I wanted to respond immediately to the children's interest and excitement in storms. I have found that if I wait a day or two before sending the family discussion sheet home, the moment has passed and the children no longer have much to say. It is helpful to create a short letter that parents can easily understand and that goes home the same day as the in-class discussion so that the children's ideas remain fresh. It is also effective to have the parents and children simply talk and tell stories at home without the complication of writing down any text, and the open-ended activity of drawing the story is developmentally appropriate for all my children.

At least 16 of my 20 students typically return the page the next day, and it is not uncommon to have all 20 children bring their sheet back to share.

With our scripted reading curriculum, we are always pressed for time, but I want all interested children to share their story in class. Sharing the story with their parents at home helps the children hone their storytelling abilities. The practice with the parent and using the drawing to guide them makes for a richer, more complete, and concise story. Our in-class sharing goes quickly and the class remains attentive looking at the drawings and listening to the stories told in Spanish, the students' primary language. As each child shares his or her story with the class, I turn this into a dictation activity as I write down their words on a big piece of paper.

The two samples of student work that follow were done by two girls in my kindergarten classroom, Angela and Mariana. Angela is 6 years old. She is a serious, quiet, and mature student. The high standards she has for herself have made her one of the top readers in class. She is fluent in Spanish and is at the early intermediate level in English, having just starting to learn English in kindergarten. Mariana is almost 6 years old. She is an excellent student who actively participates in class discussions. She is excited about school and is a naturally quick learner. She is highly articulate in Spanish and functioning at the intermediate level in English.

In these samples of student work from the home-school storm homework page, both children successfully take the theme of storms and link it to a very personal family event. The two samples show how the girls are beginning to take important risks in the classroom that will help them grow in their first and second language.

Validating Children's Experiences

Angela shared the following narrative and storm drawing (see Figure 7.1) with the class as I wrote down her words:

> *Yo fui a la pulga y luego nos agarró la tormenta. Después de eso corrimos y fuimos a mi carro. Y nos fuimos de la pulga.*
> I went to the flea market and the storm caught us. Then we ran and went to my car. And we left the flea market.

Angela began sharing her story after I asked, *"Qué pasó en tu dibujo?"* (What happened in your drawing?) She stopped after each sentence as if finished with her story. Each time she stopped, I prompted her with a question such as "And then what happened?" or "And after that?" to get more details about her storm experience. She did not elaborate on her own, although she had raised her hand and volunteered to share her story with the class. She seemed more comfortable answering my questions than sharing her story unassisted. This is typical of Angela's class partici-

Figure 7.1. Angela's Storm Drawing and Writing

pation. She rarely speaks in class discussions unless directly answering a question that I have asked. Other children at this age may speak out of turn or off topic but Angela never does. Possibly because of her shyness she feels supported by having a direct question to answer, or possibly due to her perfectionism she doesn't want to venture beyond exactly what I as the teacher want the discussion to be about. Her drawing is quite detailed but her retelling of the event is sparse.

Angela's drawing, entitled "At the Flea Market," is full of details of the market and the moment that her family was caught in the storm. We see her with her family getting soaked by the rain as they leave. She and her mother have an umbrella but they are still getting wet. The straight and slightly down-turned mouths of her family members show us the disappointment they felt this day. Not only are they getting wet, but their special family outing has been ruined by the storm. In the background, she shows us the fruit and clothing stands at the flea market also being pelted with rain from the dark storm clouds. The cars and stands in the background have clearly been drawn by someone other than Angela. I later learned that she and her mother worked together on the drawing.

Family outings to the flea market are a popular weekend activity for many of my students. Children often tell me on Monday morning, *"Maestra, fuimos a la pulga."* (Teacher, we went to the flea market.) This particular market is a favorite in the Latino community because of the products they sell and the mariachi entertainment offered in the market's center. It is reminiscent of Sunday afternoons in a small-town plaza in Mexico. Families often spend the afternoon doing the week's produce shopping, picking up some clothing or toys, and enjoying a meal while they listen to live music. Angela shared not only a storm story that goes with our class theme but also chose to share a favorite family activity with particular cultural significance.

A few days later I spoke with Maria, Angela's mother, and I learned that Angela was adamant about telling her flea market story even though her father thought she should draw something else. He didn't think that I would know what "the flea" was and he wanted to protect her from a potentially embarrassing situation with her teacher. In Spanish, a flea market is referred to as simply "the flea" and her father doubted that I would know what it was. Although I am fluent in Spanish, many families are surprised to discover how familiar I am with Mexican immigrant life even though I do not share that cultural background. I understand now why the clothing and fruit stands were drawn in the background by an adult. Her mother said that she drew them to make sure that I would know that Angela was referring to a market when she said "the flea."

I was surprised that Angela would risk not being understood by me. She is such a perfectionist and can become disappointed and frustrated when something isn't done correctly. Seeing her take this risk made me realize that she and I had begun to develop a more trusting relationship. She knew that even if I didn't know what she was talking about when she said "the flea," I would accept her story just the same. She felt confident that if I didn't understand her, I would still not judge her. She knew that I would not make her feel like she had done something wrong. I would make it my responsibility to understand her and her story with respectful questions.

Validating Children's Emotions

Mariana shared the following story and drawing (see Figure 7.2) and I wrote down her words:

> *Yo y mi hermana y mi mami no sabíamos como era la tormenta y mi papi estaba trabajando. Nosotros estabamos desesperando y mi papi se estaba mojando. Desesperabamos por la tormenta.*

Figure 7.2. Mariana's Storm Drawing and Writing

Me and my sister and my mom didn't know what the storm was like and my dad was working. We were anxious and my dad was getting wet. We were anxious because of the storm.

Mariana launched right into her story when she came to the front of the class, with almost no prompting from me. I even had to ask her to repeat herself so that I could check my dictation since she spoke so quickly. She normally speaks at a thoughtful, measured pace so I wasn't prepared for her quick, almost nervous delivery. At first, I thought I heard her say "*esperando*" (waiting). But when she said "*desesperabamos*" (we were anxious) in the next sentence, I realized that she was probably repeating the same word. I stopped and asked her if she had said "*desesperando*" in the previous sentence as well. She told me she had said "*desesperando,*" so I went back and changed my dictation.

Mariana's story and drawing show her at home with her mother and sister while her father is out working during a storm. She split her drawing into a top and bottom section, each showing the clear physical separation of her family. The upper half shows her home and the lower portion shows her father outside at another location. Mariana, her mother, and her little sister look out the windows of the house, wondering when her father will come home and if he is safe in the storm. Both she and her mother have their mouths open, possibly surprised by the storm or gasping at its strength. Their expressions may also relate to the concern Mariana has for her father, which comes across clearly in her story when she says, "*desesperabamos*," which literally translates as "we despaired." Her younger sister is smiling, possibly showing that she is too young to understand the worrisome situation in the same way as Mariana. The concern that Mariana felt for her father and her separation from him comes through clearly in the drawing and her narrative.

Later, when I spoke with Jacqueline, Mariana's mother, about the drawing and story, she told me how close Mariana is to her father. Every day Mariana looks forward to the time they spend together when he gets home from work and how she is disappointed if this doesn't happen for some reason. Her father works for the city and his primary responsibility during storms is to clean up fallen tree limbs and cut down damaged trees and limbs. Whenever there is a storm, her father works longer, more sporadic hours and arrives at home more tired than usual. Strong storms represent a disruption in the quality time Mariana gets to spend with her father and also cause her to worry about her father's well-being.

Mariana shares intense emotions in her story. She expresses her disappointment at not being with her father, desperation as she worries about his safety, and anxiety at not being able to do anything. Mariana could have drawn a generic picture of her family in a storm to avoid opening up to us, but she chose to share her inner emotional world. Mariana must have felt comfortable and safe enough to expose her home life in this way to our group.

Up to this point in the school year, Mariana had always been a competent writer in terms of spelling and mechanics, but her stories were usually simple and not interesting. Soon after sharing her storm story, though, her journals began to take on a completely different tone. She began to include more details related to emotions and opinions rather than a basic retelling of events. Sharing her storm story allowed her to expose her emotions for the first time with the class. She then felt comfortable to continue to tell her stories from a personal, emotional perspective in her journal.

CULTURALLY RESPONSIVE TEACHING AND STUDENTS' STORIES

Angela's and Mariana's stories provide insights into what is most important in their lives. Both girls show not just how they were affected by the storm but how their entire family was affected. For Angela, the storm ruined an enjoyable family outing. For Mariana, the storm meant her father would not be with her. From each story we get a sense of the storm taking something very important away—special time with family members. In sharing these stories in class, each girl took a risk and each felt safe doing so because they knew that they would be listened to and that their personal experience would be valued in my classroom. Looking at what the girls shared, I know that I have established enough trust with them to move them further academically, especially in learning the new language of English.

Using culturally responsive teaching through personal stories helped the students get to this place of respect and trust in my classroom. I also encouraged them to use Spanish in telling their stories, which allowed them to share freely. If I had required them to use only English, a language they felt less comfortable in, this might have led them to self-censor their ideas. Angela may have also given us an even more bare-bones retelling of her experience at the flea market and Mariana may have been unable to express her intense emotions as completely in English. By asking the parents to participate in the storytelling in Spanish in this homework activity, I created an important social and language link between home and school that helps support the social and language learning of my students. They need to know that what they do and experience at home is valued in the classroom. Maintaining the children's primary language and creating a link between the home and school also helps me understand and validate my students' cultural heritage. Since my cultural background is different from theirs, this is essential for creating strong personal relationships with my students. Without using culturally responsive teaching, I may not have known these students as closely as I have and created the personal relationships that allow me to support their linguistic and academic development.

As a teacher, I too miss the opportunity to get to know what is important for my students. This is often hard to do when the push to get through the curriculum is so strong. But completing the activities of our scripted language arts curriculum without any modifications is a very unresponsive way of teaching that doesn't adequately meet my teaching needs or the learning needs of my students. Even though our required language arts curriculum provides home-school activities and links that appear to have a foundation in culturally responsive teaching, they aren't nearly as effective or meaningful as the personal story activities I send home with my students. My activities are always based on my observations of what grabs the students' interest in the literature. I respond directly to what the children get excited about, not forcing them to talk about what our mandated curriculum says they should be interested in. Using only what is provided in the curriculum would result in lifeless, dead-end discussions that would further distance my students from the curriculum instead of actively engaging them.

When my students become actively and confidently engaged in school, they open up and take academic risks. They participate more in discussions and their language flourishes. Their Spanish vocabulary grows and they are able to express more and more complex ideas as their knowledge of the world expands. The children can then use this solid base of language and experience in Spanish to experiment with learning English with less fear of making mistakes and being criticized. Personal stories in my classroom are critical for promoting multilingual learning for my students, and for me to remain energized and engaged with our language arts curriculum and my students.

REFERENCE

Au, K. H. (2006). *Multicultural issues and literacy achievement.* Mahwah, NJ: Lawrence Erlbaum Associates.

Chapter 8

The Book After a Book Project: Aspects of Teaching English as a Foreign Language

INAS DEEB AND VALERIE JAKAR

Inas Deeb is a teacher trainer and English language counselor at the Pedagogical Center in East Jerusalem. She develops and organizes professional teacher training programs and projects for English teachers in East Jerusalem. Inas is interested in promoting meaningful language learning through communicative and interactive activities that develop learners' thinking skills and self-reflective learning. In her current doctoral research, she has researched how Israeli Jewish and Arab children think about social categories and about the social world.

Valerie Jakar is a sociolinguist and teacher educator at the David Yellin Academic College of Education in Jerusalem, Israel. She organizes professional development programs for teachers in Israel and East Jerusalem. Valerie is interested in the role of story in promoting second-language literacy, crosscultural communication, dialogue, and understanding "the other." She has worked for many years to bridge the political and social gap between Israeli Jews, Israeli Arabs, and Palestinians through the use and practice of English language skills. Valerie has long been active in professional organizations such as TESOL and UNICEF.

INTRODUCTION

THIS IS AN account of our initial investigation into the efficacy of professional development courses for teachers of English to young learners who are native speakers of Hebrew and Arabic. We focus on the ways that literacy skills are introduced, with special reference to a particular literacy practice, the "book after a book" project, which the teachers implemented with our young learners' classes (grades 3–6). The phrase "book after a book" is the literal translation from the Hebrew term, and its origin is unknown.

Over the past few years, in our capacities as teacher educators and counselors, we have organized several year-long courses in aspects of teaching English as an additional or foreign language. Under the auspices of the Ministry of Education, Israel, the Hebrew University of Jerusalem (NCJW) together with the Jerusalem Municipality, and the Center for Educational Technology (CET) we have conducted pre-service and in-service programs for teachers on current methodology in the field of TESOL (teaching English to speakers of other languages). Most of the participating teachers were themselves learners of English as a second or foreign language, as is one of the writers of this chapter. Important goals of the programs were always to assist the teachers' and their students' language awareness, and to develop literacy practices among the students who were all either Arabic or Hebrew speakers.

The In-Service and Pre-Service Programs

Teachers attending the programs were required to implement the newly "acquired" methodologies in their classes. We also visited their schools and provided pedagogical guidance and personal support to the teachers working on their implementation procedures. Occasionally, we acted as mediators or advocates with the school principals to ensure that the teachers put into effect the sometimes elaborate and splendid activities they had prepared. The process was arduous for both trainers and participants, but toward the end of each school year, teachers began to take great pride in their work, even to the extent of inviting parents to view displays of pupils' products.

A chance meeting with a former participant, though, led us to discover that very few of the many activities that we introduced had remained in their programs. So, in reflecting on the value of our work, we asked ourselves, "What practices did the participants retain after the initial implementations, and why?" Via an informal questionnaire and observations, we collected our preliminary data. We also visited schools and engaged in interviews and focus group discussions with teachers to strengthen our inquiry. One of the main elements we investigated was the use of story and story books in the language learning program for the young learners' classes and the concomitant literacy practices that we had promoted in the courses.

Our Population

Since English is considered an important tool for academic achievement in today's world, our public educational system includes compulsory English studies from the middle elementary grades through high school. Hebrew speakers officially begin studying English as a foreign or additional language in grade 3, up to 2 years after they have begun reading and writing in their native tongue. English lessons in many Arabic-speaking schools begin in first grade. This phenomenon is a remnant of an earlier age, when schools for Arabic-speaking children were under the authority of British rule in the region, and the prestigious schools, even to this day, use English as the language of instruction for the brightest students. The Arabic speakers today use vernacular Arabic for spoken communication in their homes and wider society. At the beginning of their school education, they must learn classical Arabic, which is the prestige code and the only accepted written variety in their society, and which functions almost as an additional language. This diglossic situation (see, e.g., Ferguson, 1959) imposes a burden on young learners from the outset of their school careers and is compounded by the added "imposition" of an English-language curriculum. Within this complicated multilingual context, we developed pre-service and in-service courses for teachers who are primarily native speakers of Arabic or Hebrew.

TEFL as a Descriptor

We refer to the teaching of English in the two communities as TEFL (Teaching English as a Foreign Language), which indicates a distinction from the type and contexts of instruction in TESL (Teaching English as a Second Language) that is practiced in countries where the native or official language is a variety of English (as in the United Kingdom, the United States, or other areas). However, in our region, gone are the days when the only exposure to the sounds and the script of English were in the classroom. In the current global economy and media, students' exposure to English is becoming increasingly broad, rendering English an additional language rather than a completely foreign language. Furthermore, since proponents of World Englishes (see, e.g., Kachru, 1985) and the ELF (English as a Lingua Franca) movement (Seidlhofer, 2004) would contend that a local variety of English may be acknowledged as an acceptable code for all but official or international purposes, the ELL of the past (a "native-speaker" variety) may soon give way to a local English for pedagogical purposes. This variety would be the English-language model of the teachers who are primarily native speakers of Hebrew or Arabic.

For the present, however, British or American "standard" English is considered the preferred prestige variety for use in the classroom, although few teachers in our elementary schools are able to represent it authentically. We will, therefore, maintain the term "TEFL" as the descriptor of our current practice in the region.

LITERACY AND TEFL DEVELOPMENT

Our linking of emergent literacy and foreign language learning is influenced by three frameworks: Taylor (1997), whose work on family literacies and story book reading led us to consider our local situation in a fresh light; Hornberger (1990), who has clarified and systematized thinking and research about biliteracy; and Weinstein (1992), whose pedagogical approach and practical materials have inspired a generation of local teachers in both our Hebrew- and Arabic-speaking groups. Most of the research on literacy is, however, related to first-language or bilingual contexts, where the language learning goal is for social and survival purposes as well as academic competence. We believe, nevertheless, that the principles of general literacy skills should be upheld for foreign language learners, too. They should become confident in engaging with texts, both orally and in writing and reading, and understand the language they are using in terms of its power, purpose, and meanings.

Literacy, even for foreign language learners, is not just "learning to read and write." We have tried to generate the principle that learners should always be aware of a purpose in using the new language and must understand the language they are using. We have tried to convey to teachers the importance of developing new language learners' literacy skills from an early age by ensuring that they understand the language they use, experience effective use of the language, and feel the personal and affective value of the writing and reading activities.

Some Practical Examples

We offer three examples of ways we promoted the integration of TEFL literacy and language learning with our local teachers. None of these examples is foreign language learning–specific, and therefore each requires that teachers give additional linguistic support, which may include the use of the first language for explanation or discussion purposes, or scaffolding (i.e., added input or information provided, again in the first language, if necessary). The first example concerns writing practice with a purpose. We repeatedly encouraged teachers to employ writing activities that engaged children in real and meaningful learning experiences. Many of our writing goals and strategies paralleled sociolinguistic principles of communication (see, e.g., Cohen & Olshtain, 1991), which support the notion of communicative competence, an idea that undergirds much current language learning and literacy pedagogy.

Our second practice related to reading comprehension skills. We endeavored to persuade teachers to guide students to think beyond the surface meanings of story texts and ask questions that not only elicit facts or information about story characters, but also to stimulate students' "higher-order" thinking skills. For instance, Haynes (2005) advocates employing Bloom's taxonomy (Bloom, 1956) as a paradigm for asking comprehension questions. In-depth questioning, probing, and appeal to the emotions or self-identification all require an engagement and investment in a foreign language, even with early learners, and this process helps language learners internalize an understanding of the new language.

Our third practice involved using story books for reading aloud, reading collectively, and exploration and creative thinking. We were careful, though, to keep in mind some of the criticisms of story book use by scholars such as Scarborough and Dobrich (1994), who note that story book reading is not common to all cultures and social classes, and that overemphasis on story book reading can devalue the literacy practices of minority and other groups. So we emphasized with teachers that although cultural and social differences need to be explained and explicated for foreign language learners, personal, traditional, and fantasy stories are rich and fertile ground for integrating new language and literacy development.

Use of Authentic TEFL Materials for Young Language Learners

Employing materials such as children's trade books added enriching, enlightening experiences for many children in our region. Our young learners do not normally benefit from access to the colorful, meaningful story books that abound in English libraries and bookstores in the West. Children's picture books are particularly appealing to students who need visual assistance to understand the written text. These books are fruitful resources for stimulating student interest and imagination, and enable them to exercise their perception, production, and creativity in both oral and written forms.

Admittedly, today's students in our public education system use textbooks that contain short stories and other texts in a range of genres with generous, age-appropriate illustrations. The exposure to different text types is concomitant with the guidelines of Israel's National Curriculum

(*National Curriculum*, 2001) which, for the domain of "Appreciation of Language and Literature," states that "pupils appreciate literature that is written in English and through it develop sensitivity to a variety of cultures" and "pupils appreciate the nature of language [and the differences between English and other languages]." Another source of stories were "Tales My Grandfather Told Me," where "grandfather" is interchanged with "aunt," "uncle," mother," and so on. These and other kinds of stories are part of units of study introduced for teachers in multicultural education courses with a folklore focus (Jakar, 2006).

THE BOOK AFTER A BOOK PROJECT

The "book after a book" project, though requiring rigorous orientation by teachers and careful stage-by-stage monitoring of all students, can be instituted even for the youngest EFL learners. In fact, as soon as children have learned that English text requires left to right orientation, they can produce something that resembles an actual book. In the "book after a book" project, students were asked to replicate stories they had read, but to alter some details so that the story became their own. Having created a new version, they read it once more, then moved on to read their classmates' creations, or went to the library to find similar "authors." For early learners, where the text involved in the original reading materials was minimal, the production of their very own book was a momentous step in the direction of literacy in the new language. The students also illustrated their books, and although the teachers provided significant scaffolding (Berk & Winsler, 1995), the project led to a newfound sense of "ownership," always a powerful motivator for further learning.

Further, by producing their own publications, the students not only learned about text types, vocabulary, and syntax in a new language, but also about the requirements of an acceptable publication. Typical features of a publication included the title, author's name, illustrator or graphics editor, other authors involved (if, perhaps a parent assisted in the production of the book), and acknowledgments (to the original author of the trade book or to the teacher). At a further stage in students' proficiency, some students wrote a blurb about the book and a "bio" of the author, constituting the two endpapers of a designed book cover.

Two examples of the children's books show the students' use of story language and story content in English. Bushra's "The Dog and the Cat" begins with a short biographical statement, then an introduction, and finally an original story. Bushra also provided a series of careful color pencil illustrations (see Figure 8.1).

Figure 8.1. Bushra's "The Dog and the Cat" Drawing

Myself

My name is Bushra. I live in Beit Safafa. I am twelve years old. I am 145 cm tall. I like oranges, banana. I am in a class room. I hate the zoo. I slept.

Introduction

The story is about the cat and the dog. The story is very beautiful.

The Dog and the Cat

One day the cat and the dog were friends and ate and played together. The dog is a gardener. In the dark night and they sleeps alltogether into the same house. The man who has the house, gives them present to eat and drink. The dog and the cat became strong because the dog and the cat eat well. They become big. They become active in the work. At the end, the dog and the cat live in happiness. The end beautiful. of the story.

Donya's story entitled "The Woodcutter" shows how she incorporated certain English expressions in her retelling of a familiar folktale originally told to her in Arabic. Donya also illustrated her story, with one picture per page (see Figure 8.2.).

Figure 8.2. Donya's "The Woodcutter" Drawing

Myself

My name is Donya Magid. I live in Beit Safafa. I like ice cream,
bananas. I'm twelve years old. I'm 145 cm tall. I love my grandmother very much because she tell me beautiful stories for her
stories always have good ends. Yestoday she told me one.

The Woodcutter

In one day there is a poor man who has a big family. He is a
woodcutter and he always sells the trees. He sells them in the city,
and buys with the money flowers and food to his family. One day
he sat with his wife eating their lunch. It was bread and cheese.
The woodcutter said to his wife, "I hate my life. I work very hard
and there is no money enough and no strong health for work."
His wife said, "Don't be hopeless. No one knows about luck.
Maybe some day we will be very rich." The man shouted, "Which
luck, we don't have any luck."

Suddenly a cat jumps on the food and steel a piece of cheese. The man shouted to his wife and said, "This is our luck you are talking about?" Then he ran after the cat. The cat ran away from the woodcutter and go into a wall. Then the man started to dig in the wall searching for the cat. While was he digging he said, "After a short time I will catch the bad cat." Suddenly, he found a pot, he opened it and found gold. The woodcutter returned home and said to his wife, "You are a good wife, our luck comes. I found gold, we became rich people." After that, he built a beautiful house. They live in the house happily. Do you see how the stories of my grandmother are beautiful? Oh!!! Yes.

Through the production of their books, students gained knowledge of several critical literacy skills in a new language:

- Sequencing story events
- Expanding story events
- Changing story endings
- Choosing new titles
- Comparing story characters
- Comparing story characters with real-life characters

These and other strategies helped students "own" their texts, and supported their dialogue and negotiation with peers and teachers about the content and form of their stories and books.

The Power of Story Texts and Formats

When student products are the result of a creative process (admittedly based on an existing text or story) as in the "book after a book" project, they must nevertheless be accurate, and with language levels that are comprehensible to their peers for them to become part of the class or grade library. This is assuming, of course, that the information presented is valid, and the language employed is sufficiently accurate and appropriate for peer-reading. It therefore behooves teachers to determine criteria for task production and insist on adherence to those criteria. Clear writing, accurate spelling, and some illustration of ideas were required for a work to be "published," and for all concerned, norms of publishing needed to be upheld. Thus, for example, even at the Foundation level for beginners (*National Curriculum*, 2001), students need to know that the author's name must appear, along with the date of publication, the names of collaborating writers, and the publisher's name and place of operation. While the students were honing their products into shape, attending to the rubric set by their teacher, they also gained literacy skills experientially. We have found this to be an optimum way to learn, be it in the first language or in subsequent languages.

Our learners were not restricted in the types of stories they could emulate. They were encouraged to create their books based on traditional stories, such as "Cinderella" or "Aladdin," that they might have learned in their native language, or by adapting teachers' read-alouds of big book versions of story books. Eric Carle's (1979) The Very Hungry Caterpillar was popular with the students because of its unique presentation format; there are holes cut in the book to resemble the work of a nibbling creature. This book lent itself to a variety of TEFL literacy practices and language building—paying attention to repetition and sequence in an exciting story and to a range of meaningful vocabulary situated in recognizable semantic sets, both of which can be replicated or adapted by students. This delightful story also exposes TEFL readers to issues of nutrition, science, colors, and the days of the week. When student (re-)creators of this story used just one of these elements as their story base, they produced a fine reader for their peers to enjoy.

First-Language Literacy Through Foreign Language Acquisition

It must be pointed out that although some of the literacy skills introduced through projects like "book after a book" are universal, there are some with which native speakers of Arabic or Hebrew are not familiar. Only much later, in middle school, are our students introduced to phenomena such as genre (text type) and styles of writing in their own first language. Indeed, it has been found that the learning strategies and creative activities in TEFL classes also enhance native language literacy skills (see, e.g., Sanduka, 2008). In our "book after a book" project, this was attested to by several teacher participants in the in-service courses. Furthermore, production, publication, and display of a document known as a "book" is seen as a superb means of empowerment in every community. The rise in self-esteem for the students as they presented their books was clearly evident. We have found that our students' motivation to achieve increased exponentially as the students received positive feedback on their language and literacy products.

FUTURE DIRECTIONS FOR STORY AND OUR TEFL TEACHING

Our inquiry has yielded valuable data that we are still processing. We will continue to reflect on the results of the administration and distribution of an informal questionnaire, interviews, and school visits, and discussion sessions that have taken place over the last 6 years. Our observations prompt us to ask many more questions, which will constitute the next stage in our investigation. We received 66 responses to a questionnaire distributed to teachers in 55 schools. In a substantial proportion of the responses, teachers admitted that they no longer included the EFL literacy practices that they had learned about in our in-service sessions. We discovered that only two of the schools we polled actually continued to have the "book after a book" project as an integral part of their curriculum. Other schools included it occasionally as a special project. We argue, though, that occasional implementation is but a poor substitute for routine practices to support TEFL development in language and literacy. Teachers at other schools were asked why the various practices were abandoned, even though they had reported that they were productive and successful. Sample responses included:

"I couldn't do it alone."
"None of my colleagues were doing it."
"We had the new textbook and I had to get right through it."
"The principal needed me to give grades for tests so I didn't have
     time to do extra projects."

In addition, we learned from a colleague who is a specialist in literacy in Arabic that a similar project proved highly successful when he monitored it regularly but it was not continued the following year when he left the project. As another contributing factor to the difficulty of sustaining this kind of innovative TEFL work, some teachers noted that while young language learners are keen to engage in projects, their parents, not seeing a grade, worry that their children are not learning anything of value and substance.

Professional Support

It became clear to us that without the support of the school principal, whose awareness of the value of the practice was vital but often lacking, and without ongoing support from colleagues, the logistical and pedagogical constraints of such tasks are too complex and too reliant on an individual teacher's personal energy and input. In subsequent interviews and group discussion, we learned from the teachers in the two schools that continued the project that they benefited from continual support from their school principals, who acknowledged their use of "book after a book" both as a valuable TEFL literacy tool and as a valid assessment instrument. The teachers were also permitted space, time, and materials to display the students' books, along with relevant publicity—in the school community and further afield—so that there was an audience for their work.

Perpetuating the Practice

One cohort of teachers developed rubrics for final evaluation of the students' book products in cooperation with their students. While everyone in the course group was enthusiastic about this innovative step, the teachers involved did not reflect-in-action, nor did they engage in any critical evaluation of the rubrics produced and subsequently implemented. They implemented the evaluation component, assigning a grade scale for use by the class teacher for end-of-year reports, but apparently that was the end of the project.

In only one school, where the "book after a book" project is firmly established, did we note evidence of subsequent use of the books. In this school, every acceptable document, produced and "published," is incorporated into the classroom libraries. Small groups of students then read to one another, or have the story read to them by the author, the teacher, or a peer, just as with any other kind of story book. The teacher prepares task cards for each book in the library area that consist of a series of questions about the text. The students choose, read, and critique their peers' work just as they might report on the work of an established author. These practices reinforce the empowerment already conferred on these new authors.

An interesting phenomenon was pointed out to us regarding the introduction of these kinds of TEFL literacy practices. When the teachers were engaged in developing these programs in the in-service course, they were told by colleagues (class teachers of both Arabic- and Hebrew-speaking learners) that the students were demonstrating accelerated literacy skills in their regular classes (in their first language) as a result of the tasks they performed in their English classes. It is not for us to dictate how literacy skills and practices should be developed in the first-language situation, but it is clear to us that our classes on TEFL literacy skills have had language transfer benefits for students' first-language learning.

Some Causes for Concern

Many of the elementary school teachers with whom we work have minimal awareness of the purposes and the practices of TEFL literacy skills. The teachers are totally reliant on the use of the mandatory textbook, which they call "the curriculum," and which serves as the sole directive for their teaching. Their situation is reminiscent of Serebrin's (2004) comment about his in-service student teachers: ". . . any professional sense and scholarly wondering was shut down, as they resigned themselves to merely carrying out their classroom teachers' practices without question." This kind of thinking was reflected in our teachers' responses to our questionnaire.

There are other elements that are also cause for concern. After talking with the teachers who shared with us the different ways they believed they could promote TEFL language and literacy development, we realized that their perceptions differed from ours. For them, the learning of lists of vocabulary items through rote learning memorization and repetition constituted an important TEFL language and literacy practice. On one school visit, we witnessed wall displays of decontextualized pronouns, and irregular verbs with endings categorized, among pretty illustrations and paper creations (of butterflies and flowers), which bore little relation to the words displayed. While we were impressed by the aesthetics of the boardwork and visual displays, we also noted the lack of real understanding of deep TEFL learning strategies. It was little wonder that the teachers reported that, though the students had been learning for 3 years, by the time they reached fourth grade, they still could not carry on a casual conversation with a peer in English, and although they could write a short paragraph and read aloud an English text, they had little understanding of what was written and said.

Still, a challenge and an achievement for this population was story reading (aloud) and teaching their classmates the new vocabulary by imitating the teacher's story scaffolding methods. A group of innovative English teachers at one school reported important new practices: introducing reading books and stories that were not part of their textbook program, presenting and discussing new vocabulary prior to reading a text, encouraging students to write their own stories based on the characteristics of a particular story format, and writing their own stories based on a published story book. These were all unique experiences that the students had not encountered when learning Arabic or other school subjects. These and other kinds of language and literacy activities are familiar activities conducted in the first language in the West, but are rarely to be found in public education in our region.

FINAL REFLECTIONS

It is clear that the implementation of new and innovative practices to promote story and TEFL development in language and literacy must be seen as a work-in-progress. It is important to introduce an attractive project, implement a cycle of activities, and then work to establish that practice permanently. From other data and discussion with teachers, we conclude that it is not the authorities alone that prevent the implementation and perpetuation of a practice that has such potential. We ourselves as teacher educators omitted to establish or provide strategies for the aftermath or outcomes of practices such as "book after a book." Teachers were not given sufficient guidance as to how to perpetuate and exploit the use of the final product of the personally published books.

We are now convinced that by imbuing the teachers with an understanding of new and powerful TEFL language and literacy practices, we can help promote meaningful new language use and appreciation of English. We will look further at strategies that teachers employ to develop their students' TEFL development, and we will investigate the ways in which students create story products to demonstrate their abilities and capabilities, and how this work influences their other TEFL learning patterns. With regard to the relationship between stories and story books in TEFL language and literacy practices, we need to examine how rigorous a teacher should be in requiring perfect production. What are the positive and what are the negative effects on the EFL learning process when students are required to produce a flawless presentation in a foreign language? How can teachers ensure that every student gets to publish and display? What criteria must be established to ensure equity among the classes of learners?

We are gratified that some schools (and some individual teachers) retained the TEFL story practices and their development at least to a certain extent. These teachers are also prepared to disseminate information about their practices, and have expressed an interest in researching their teaching to deepen their understanding and improve their practice. We hope to involve these teachers in our future inquiry into this compelling area of our work.

REFERENCES

Berk, L. E., & Winsler, A. (1995). *Scaffolding children's learning: Vygotsky and early childhood education.* NAEYC Research into Practice Series, Volume 7. Washington, DC: National Association for the Education of Young Children.

Bloom, B. S. (Ed.). (1956). *Taxonomy of educational objectives: The classification of educational goals.* New York: Longmans, Green.

Carle, E. (1979). *The very hungry caterpillar.* New York: Philomel Books.

Cohen, A. D., & Olshtain, E. (1991). Teaching speech act behavior to nonnative speakers. In M. Celce-Murcia (Ed.), *An introduction to teaching English as a second or foreign language* (2nd Ed.) (pp. 167–180). Cambridge, MA: Newbury House/ Harper & Row.

Haynes, J. (2005). Bloom's taxonomy and English language learners. Retrieved September 8, 2008, from http://www.everythingesl.net/inservices/blooms_ taxonomy_language_learn_16902.php

Hornberger, N. (1990). Creating successful contexts for bilingual literacy. *Teachers College Record, 92*(2), 212–229.

Jakar, V. S. (2006). Knowing the other through multicultural projects. In G. Becket & P.C. Miller (Eds.), *Project-based second and foreign language education: Past, present, and future* (pp. 181–194). Chicago: Age Publishing Inc.

Kachru, B. (1985). Standards, codification and sociolinguistic realism. In R. Quirk (Ed.), *English in the world* (pp. 11–34). Cambridge, UK: Cambridge University Press.

National curriculum. (2001). Jerusalem, Israel: Ministry of Education.

Sanduka, Y. (2008). The Relationship between phonological awareness and reading acquisition. *Elkarmeh* (pp. 69–71). Jerusalem, Israel: David Yellin College Press (Arabic speakers' division).

Scarborough, H. S., & Dobrich, W. (1994). On the efficacy of reading to preschoolers. *Developmental Review, 14(3),* 245–302.

Seidlhofer, B. (2004). Research perspectives on teaching English as a lingua franca. *Annual Review of Applied Linguistics, 24,* 209–239.

Serebrin, W. (2004). Melissa's story: Bridging theory/practice. *Canadian Journal of Educational Administration and Policy, 32,* 1–19. Retrieved February 2, 2008, from http://www.umanitoba.ca/publications/cjeap/articles/noma/melissastory. html

Taylor, D. (1997). (Ed.). *Many families, many literacies: An international declaration of principles.* Portsmouth, NH: Heinemann.

Weinstein, G. (1992). *Stories to tell our children.* New York: Heinle & Heinle, Inc.

PART III

STORIES
and
CHILDREN'S
LITERACY
DEVELOPMENT

Chapter 9

"Once Upon a Time There Was a . . . ": Forms and Functions of Story Dictation in Preschool

JEFF DAITSMAN

Jeff Daitsman currently works at a suburban Chicago early care and education center, where he runs a naptime classroom for preschool children who cannot sleep. He also assists children with special needs throughout the day. In the past he had volunteered nationally with the American Red Cross and Stolen Lives Project, caring for children who had recently undergone traumatic experiences. He holds a Basic Certificate in Child Development from Truman College, where he is completing his A.A.S.

Dice Cream by Lionel

Ice cream. Dice cream. Dice cream? What? Dice cream is yucky. Yucky? Yucky. Yucky. Yucky! Yucky! Yucky! Yucky! Yucky. Yucky. Use that.

Each time I read back 3-year-old Lionel's story dictation, he seemed to find his words new and fresh. He found the repetition of the word *yucky* so exciting that it became all that he would do until a distraction arose and he chose to end the story. The excitement of seeing his words put onto paper engaged Lionel, drawing him in and helping him build that ever-so-difficult bridge between the spoken word and the written word.

I LEARNED IN my studies in Child Development at Truman College about the art of story dictation and decided that I could make this a small part of my curriculum in my first full school year teaching preschool. From Lev Vygotsky (1978), I knew the value of play in development and that ". . . play contains all developmental tendencies in a condensed form and is itself a major source of development" (p. 102). I found children who were particularly imaginative players and would approach them and ask if they would like to tell me a story. If they were agreeable, they dictated their story to me, I wrote it down mostly verbatim, and then read it back so the children and their peers could hear it. Sometimes I would read it back at group time to the entire class, and sometimes to a smaller group of children with whom the child was playing. The children humored me with this, but I found myself approaching them more than they approached me to dictate a story.

I began to wonder if story dictation was really developmentally appropriate. If the children weren't interested, then how much value could it hold for their social, language, and play development? Was this activity one that was really in adherence with a play-based curriculum? I thought about Vivian Paley's (1981, 1998) children and their love of story dictation. Why didn't my children feel the same connection to their stories? The problem, as I would discover, was that my children were not truly engaged in the process.

Kamii and Devries (2004) describe the Piagetian idea that ". . . it is in interpersonal situations that the child feels an obligation to be coherent" (p. 16). Paley (1990) applies this concept to story dictation, stressing the value of children connecting their stories to their play: "The play and the stories and the talk nourish one another and translate into ever more logical thought and social effectiveness" (p. 21). I wasn't allowing the children this interpersonal engagement. I needed to make story dictation a more central aspect of my curriculum. Ann Gadzikowski (2007) states, "One of the best ways to build on and share stories while developing a strong sense of community in your classroom is to act them out or dramatize them" (p. 62).

It wasn't until we began dramatizing the stories that I began to feel this sense of community. It was then that my classroom became a place where children's stories came to life. With never more than 10 children on any given day, I transcribed dictations for more than 60 children in our center over the course of the year. I found that although each child is unique in how he or she dictates stories, there are also common threads in the themes that the children address.

Some children find it important to connect their stories to drawings and other visual stimuli. When I saw this desire, I encouraged the children to pursue it and expand their media of expression. Acting out the stories was one of the means I provided, and it allowed them to make the connection that Vygotsky (1978) describes when he states that ". . . make-believe play, drawing, and writing can be viewed as different moments in an essentially unified process of development of written language . . ." (p. 116).

Many of the children used their stories to come to terms with difficult emotions. Erik Erikson (1963) points out how "playing it out" helps children work through difficult experiences, comparing it to the adult process of "talking it out" (p. 222). By dramatizing violent or painful themes in their stories, the children seemed to gain a greater degree of control over what they were feeling.

The children also used the story dictation process to explore gender stereotypes and what it means to be boys and girls. They experimented with a variety of advanced technology as well, utilizing story dictation as a means through which to expand their understanding of the technology I provided for them. I found story dictation and dramatization to be an excellent method of teaching a wide variety of early childhood competencies, including, but not limited to, literacy.

Too often, current literacy education focuses on understanding the basic mechanics of being able to read and write. There is not enough emphasis on the fact that written language is just that—a form of language. As a result, the content of the writing tends to get lost. Based on their research on first-grade writers, Stribling and Kraus (2007) encourage teachers to ". . . challenge this linear model in favor of a more complex approach that encourages young writers to explore content at the same time they are making sense of mechanics" (p. 15). Story dictation is an excellent means of integrating the two. Over time, the preschool children began to notice exactly what I was doing with my pen and paper and began to emulate it, coming naturally to the mechanical aspects of writing when they were ready for it. I learned through this process that story, when combined with play, can be a very powerful stimulus for children's language and literacy development.

FROM STORY DICTATION TO STORY DRAMA

In my classroom, 4-year-olds Joshua and Steven were two of only three children dictating stories during the month of September. Then, in early October, they dictated a story together entitled "Pictures." Once we were situated and ready to transcribe, I simply said as I said to all the children, "Tell me your story."

Pictures

Once upon a time there was a Blue Lake that lived in a fish tank
that goed in a Halloween house. And then there came a ghost.
And he wanted to say, "Hi." And he was friendly. And Blue Lake
did say, "Hi." And then Mr. Jeff came and ate up the ghost and
Blue Lake. And then Blue Lake killed him and then they lived
happily ever after. The End

The day before, the children had taken photographs of our classroom,
which I developed overnight, and then the next day, I put Velcro on the
back of the photos so that the children could affix them to a felt board.
Joshua and Steven used these photographs as a springboard for their "Pictures" story.

This combination of the oral (telling the story) with the visual (looking at the photographs and my writing their story down) set the tone for
Joshua's first experiences with story dictation. Two days later, during a
portion of a new dictated story, Joshua referenced some photographs of
children with their families on the wall:

He came back and then they had a picnic. And they took pictures.
And then one of them was the happiest one. This one that I'm
touching. And then the next part they went to the pool and they
got in the water . . .

Three weeks later, Joshua's next story took his need to combine visual
stimuli with his stories a step further. After he dictated his story, he asked
me to draw a picture of the spiders for him, to which I responded, "Why
don't you draw them?" and handed him the pen.

Ca Ca

Once upon a time there was a little boy. And then there was lots
of spiders. And then the next thing that happened was there was
a guy that fighted him.

Nearly all of Joshua's stories thereafter included illustrations. Joshua
needed there to be more than simply telling a story and having it read
back to the group. It took me nearly a month to find a good way to support Joshua's need to combine story dictation and drawing, and when I
did so, more children wanted to do story dictation.

It was partly seeing Joshua's strong desire to make his story come to
life by adding the illustration to "Ca Ca," and partly rewatching a video

of Vivian Paley (Paley, 2002) discussing the art of story drama that inspired me to begin having children act out their stories. I had attempted it twice over the summer and had been disappointed with the outcome. But with Vivian Paley's method fresh in my mind, I attempted it once more.

I decided that if I truly wanted to make this a multisensory experience, there were a number of changes I needed to make. So I decided to xxxxx a list for children to put their names on if they wanted to tell me a story, and I also began using larger, more visible print when I wrote the stories down. Next to the list was a small table with only two chairs that I designated as our dictation table. I also began restricting the children to a single page so that it would be short enough to hold their attention when acting the stories out. Later on, during group time, I informed the children that we were going to put on a play with their stories. I used masking tape to tape off a rectangle on the floor as Vivian Paley suggests, and explained to the children that this would be our stage. Despite needing to be patched up several times, the rectangle remained on the floor all year.

As the children dictated more stories in November, our story drama evolved and changed. For instance, after 4-year-old Linda dictated the following story, she asked me if she could take a bow.

Cinderella and the Beauty's Heart of the Beast

Cinderella went walking and walking until she went to a castle. And then she went walking to pick up her baby from the hospital. And then her baby wanted to go home so she went home. And she play with her little baby. And then when it was time to eat you know. And then the baby had to go to sleep. And then her mama went to sleep right next to her. And then the mom went to go pick up the baby at 2:00. And then she went home to go sleep. The End.

I told Linda that she could bow, and 4-year-old Shauna then took us a step further following the enactment of her story that same day.

The Princess and the Prince

Once upon a time there was a princess who had a little dolly. And it was very cute. And it was a puppy. And it was very very very cute. And she liked to sleep with it. And it had very soft fur. And she had a little dolly kitten. And it was very cute. And she had a little small cow. And it was very very very cute. And it had a little it had black and white. And he had a cute beard. A little cute beard. And she married a prince. THE END

Linda had acted the role of the princess in Shauna's story, and Shauna, as if inspired by Linda's bow following her own story, asked Linda to join her in bowing at the end of their enactment of Shauna's story. The tradition that Linda started remained, and eventually expanded to the audience of children sometimes adding applause during the bowing.

STORY DICTATION AND CHILDREN'S EMOTIONS

The children were often motivated to dictate their stories and act them out because of the emotional content and message of their stories. In mid-November, Linda dictated a story about Cinderella giving birth and the baby needing surgery in a hospital.

Cinderella

Cinderella went to the castle to get some food. And then she sat down to eat. And she went to go to the baby. And she lifter her baby up and she fed him some food. And then she went to the baby hospital and he got poked and he got a check-up. And then her baby got surgery. And then her mom got to the hospital because she die and got sicked. And then the baby cry and cry. And then the king came and said, "What's the matter?" And then the baby told the king a story and the Mom died and he cried. Because the Mom died and then the Dad said, "Oh my gosh!" The End.

Linda, like all young children who are often anxious about illness and death, thought a lot about the content of her story. But by telling and playing out a story about a hospital, Linda faced her fears and her limited knowledge of illness and hospitals.

Other children used stories as well to help them come to terms with difficult emotions. Four-year-old Jeremy sometimes became frustrated when things did not go his way. We had been dramatizing story dictations for several weeks before Jeremy's first visit to my room in mid-November. Jeremy declined to act in any of the six stories produced that day. But after the first few stories, Jeremy allowed himself to be entertained by the performance. During the next several story enactments, Jeremy continued to be mesmerized by the performances, but he also continued to decline to participate, until one day in early December, 3-year-old Gabriella told an untitled story that included Jeremy's name:

> A Spider-Man. Jeremy. Dinosaur. Ticket. Poopy. Stinky butt. Shut up. Stupid. Hin.

He didn't act in Gabriela's story, but Jeremy did act in every other story put on that day. A few days later, Jeremy dictated his own story for the first time.

Santa Gives Presents Out

> I want Santa in my story. And I want some reindeers in mine. That's it.

The act of story dictation gave Jeremy an opportunity to be in control. For this child who had some difficulty controlling his emotions, this process gave him a chance to sit back and direct what happened before him. Jeremy participated in several other stories that day, but for his own story he just wanted to watch. He became the consummate playwright and director, satisfied to create a work of theatrical art that, once completed, he could simply sit back and observe. For Jeremy, the written story didn't need anything more than a cast of characters because the performance would speak for itself. He took control when his peers began performing the story. He showed them where to stand, and how the reindeer needed to be in front of Santa because Santa was in the sleigh. He had a vision in his mind and seemed to have more control over it by seeing it played out before him than by being part of it himself.

STORY DICTATION AND GENDER STEREOTYPES

In mid-December, 3-year-old Mary's story, "Ariel," was a fairly typical story for her during this period.

Ariel

> Once upon a time and there was a princess. And bunnies came. More bunny rabbits. More bunny rabbits. Sheep. More sheeps. More sheeps. And more sheeps. And more sheepses. And more bunny rabbits. And more sheepses. And more sheeps. And bunny

rabbits. And more sheeps. More sheepses. More sheepses. Ariel. And THE END.

On the same day that Mary dictated this story, she portrayed Santa Claus in a story dictated by Joshua immediately prior to acting out her own story. However, when Jeremy requested that he play Ariel, Mary was very adamant that Ariel must be played by a girl. This started a debate in the classroom about whether boys should be allowed to play girls and girls be allowed to play boys. The children concluded that since it was just pretend, it was fine for boys and girls to take on opposite-sex roles in the stories. Jeremy tended to prefer to play female parts in the story dramatizations and acted in more "girl" stories than "boy" stories. Jeremy took pride in the idea that boys could be pretend mermaids, and for the following month and a half, the majority of Jeremy's stories contained mermaids before he began expanding to other "girl" themes.

Snow White and Sleeping Beauty

Once upon a time there was a hot Snow White. Then came Sleeping Beauty. Then The End.

Jeremy was not the first student in my classroom to counter gender stereotypes with his story dictation. Several months earlier, Mary had dictated her third story, "Batman's Story," the day before Halloween.

Batman's Story

Once upon a time it has a Superman. And Batman killed him away. And then he put him in jail. He locked him up in a cage. And then he saw the pumpkin. And then a mouse come in a cage and a mouse come sneaking on. And then he fall down. And then he eat him up, saying, "Yummy lunch. Yummy lunch. Yummy yummy mouse lunch." And then the Batman locked him up and he started fight him up. And then he started to fight. And then a monster came and everyone go home. And then a dinosaur come with the monster. And then jump jump in a house in a roof. And then fall down and kid say, "Very scared." And THE END.

I had made story dictation a part of my classroom since the very start of the school year, yet prior to this day, not a single superhero story had appeared from either the boys or the girls. Only later in the year did Mary's stories gradually became less violent and become more traditionally "girly."

STORY DICTATION AND CHILDREN'S COGNITIVE DEVELOPMENT

Although this was our first superhero story of the year, it was far from the last. Often, the children's story characters related to an element of popular culture for which their only base of reference came from what they gleaned from peers. Four-year-old David's father tells me that he has never seen any Power Ranger shows or movies, but in mid-December, David dictated a story entitled "Power Rangers." In this story, he included a Purple Power Ranger, which does not actually exist on the television show.

Power Rangers

This is the story of Power Rangers. The Blue one was bigger. And the Red one was bigger too. And the Purple one was big and bigger. And the Blue one said, "There's trouble." And the Red one said, "That's not good." The Purple one didn't like that. And the Red one didn't even like it so much long. THE END

When we began casting David's story, a few children objected to the Purple Ranger. By defining the Blue and Red Rangers as "bigger," and the Purple Ranger as "big and bigger," he may have intended the Purple Ranger as a merging of the other two. If this is the case, David demonstrates knowledge of color mixing and an understanding of size relationships.

Stories can also describe relationships between numbers, and in mid-November, 3-year-old Brian's third story to be acted out illustrates children's developing sense of number and computational operations such as addition.

Star Wars

Once upon a time there was two Storm Troopers. And once upon a time there was one Darth Vader. Mary's using two of those. Once upon a time there was two more Storm Troopers. Once upon a time there was four Storm Troopers. That's the end.

I didn't notice it when Brian dictated the story, but when the children were acting it out I noticed that Brian had incorporated into his story the concept of $2 + 2 = 4$. Every story that Brian dictated incorporated numbers. I had always thought story dictation was good only (or at least primarily) for teaching literacy, but for Brian it involved teaching numeracy, a close cousin to literacy.

As the year went on, the children's stories became more developed, and their understanding of the relationship between writing and speech increased. The stories began to flow more and the children began taking an interest in writing themselves. Some children wrote their own names on their stories, while others wrote an occasional word here or there that was particularly meaningful to them. By late May, several children had taken an interest in writing their entire story and copying the words as I wrote them. Gabriella's story, "Once Upon" (see Figures 9.1 and 9.2), demonstrates how she uses the process of story dictation to practice the formation of letters.

STORY DICTATION AND TECHNOLOGY

Four-year-old Peter dictated his third story in mid-November on a day I introduced a new technology into the classroom. I brought in a small handheld digital voice recorder. The children spent a long time playing with it. When Peter had his turn, he recorded a 4-second story—"Power Rangers Are Special"—and played it back over and over as he repeated, "Now I'm done. Now this button?" Later that afternoon, Peter dictated the following story on paper:

Power Rangers

I really like Power Rangers. They're so cool because they have a ship and they have powers. They have rings too and you put your hand on something and it makes white stuff. And I think it's lasers. THE END

Peter used this process to explore new technology by connecting it with the familiar concept of story dictation.

Although voice recorders were useful, computers proved a much more powerful technological tool for story dictation. Four-year-old Shane's first experience with story dictation involved acting in stories that children had dictated as I had typed them in our computer lab. This inspired Shane to put his name on the list to dictate his own story a week later when I had set up my laptop computer with a printer at the dictation table.

While he waited for his turn that day, Shane sat down at a drawing table and made two drawings, one of a big blue face and the other a big green face, and he used these as the inspiration for his story.

[untitled]

One time there was a guy and another guy and he was all green 'cause he was really scared 'cause he saw a shark. But it wasn't

Figure 9.1. Gabriella Dictating Her "Once Upon a Time" Story to Jeff

Figure 9.2. Gabriella's "Once Upon a Time" Dictated Story

really a shark 'cause it was a costume. And one time the green guy and they went to sleep so then they came back to home. And they didn't leave by their home so they didn't like it so they went back to their other home. 'Cause they had two homes.

As I typed Shane's dictation, he looked back and forth between his drawing, my typing on the keyboard, and the emerging text on the computer screen. Shane used the process of story dictation on the laptop to bring his drawing to life. His big green face leapt off the page through his story, and later, during story acting, Shane further extended his vision of his artwork.

When we were in the computer lab, the children took great joy in running over to the printer to watch their stories come out. "Here it comes," I said to the children as I sent their story dictations to the printer. "Can I press?" became Clark's question of choice as he learned which buttons were acceptable to press and when. Three-year-old Clark didn't tell a story the first time he saw the printer, but he did express interest and excitement in his own way. He took a marker from the dry-erase board and scribbled directly on the printer. The next day, Clark dictated a story on the computer.

Story Time

Here comes. Can I press. Huh? Five. Tell me a story.

Clark became interested in story dictation because of the use of computer technology, but his first story (which he would share with the group) was all about the process of story dictation. It was as if Clark started with a fascination with the end-product, and then explored the process.

Clark continued not to show any interest in story dictation using only pen and paper. Whereas Joshua loved to add illustrations to his dictated stories on paper, Clark found more power in dictated stories on the computer. In Clark's final, untitled story during the fall, he continued to demonstrate a fascination with the computer:

C-L-A-R-K spells Clark. C-L-A-R spells Jeff. That's Clark! My Daddy. Da da da da da da da. And because and my Daddy is nice.

As he stared at my fingers poised above the keyboard, Clark also looked at the letters on the keys beneath my fingers. When he first began speaking, I typed the word *See*. This confused him as he looked for the letter "c" on the screen. It took me a moment to realize that he was trying to say the letter "c" and so I corrected my mistake. When I did, it became clear to me that Clark knew something more about the process of story dictation than simply the words to facilitate the process. Clark understood that everything he said was translated into letters, which was supported by the concrete visual of my laptop keyboard. The keyboard spurred his interest in using oral language to transfer the letters on the keyboard onto the computer screen, and eventually onto paper. To start this process on a powerful note, Clark began his story by spelling the word that he knew best—his name.

STORY DICTATION—BEYOND LITERACY AND TOWARD IDENTITY

Communication is the essence of literacy, and it is when young children are at play that they have the greatest desire to communicate with their peers. As Vygotsky (1978) describes, "children's symbolic play can be understood as a very complex system of 'speech' through gestures . . ." (p. 108). As the story dictation examples from my students demonstrate, preschool children can find meaning in the written word through dictating and playing out their stories.

The process of watching their spoken words transfer immediately into written words helps children understand important functions of written language   that writing has a message, meaning, it can inform, entertain, and delight both the self as teller/writer and the audience. When the children and I "read" back their dictated stories, we checked for understanding and for possible revision, and this, too, reinforced the idea that dictation creates written texts to be negotiated and shared in a public way. I found it even more valuable, however, for me to read the dictated story to a group of the child's peers. The children then dramatized the stories, combining the benefits of story dictation with the benefits of play and enabling the words to come to life.

I also found that children gain more from this process than purely meaningful literacy experiences. They explore their own identity with these stories while strengthening valuable relationships with their peers through dramatization. They enhance their emotional and cognitive capabilities through experimentation and play. At the same time, they can also use this process to explore and gain experience with new communication technologies.

The use of story dictation and dramatization in the preschool classroom integrates a wide variety of learning objectives. These are the kinds of valuable experiences that instill in young children a desire to expand their means of communication as well as to learn about themselves and the world. New to teaching preschool, this was my first attempt at story dictation with children, and I learned as much about its value for children as I did about how story dictation enriches my own teaching and understanding of children.

REFERENCES

Erikson, E. H. (1963). *Childhood and society* (2nd ed.). New York: W. W. Norton.

Gadzikowski, A. (2007). *Story dictation: A guide for early childhood professionals.* St. Paul, MN: Redleaf Press.

Kamii, C., & Devries, R. (2004). *Group games in early education: Implications of Piaget's theory.* Washington, DC: NAEYC.

Paley, V. G. (1981). *Wally's stories: Conversations in the kindergarten.* Cambridge, MA: Harvard University Press.

Paley, V. G. (1990). *The boy who would be a helicopter: The uses of storytelling in the classroom.* Cambridge, MA: Harvard University Press.

Paley, V. G. (1998). *The girl with the brown crayon: How children use stories to shape their lives.* Cambridge, MA: Harvard University Press.

Paley, V. G. (2002). *Storytelling themes with Vivian Gussin Paley.* DVD. Ball State University, 2002.

Stribling, S. M., & Kraus, S. M. (2007). Content and mechanics: Understanding first grade writers. *Voices of Practitioners.* Retrieved June 4, 2008, from http://journal.naeyc.org/btj/vp/VoicesStriblingKraus.pdf

Vygotsky, L. S. (1978). *Mind in society: The development of higher psychological processes.* Cambridge, MA: Harvard University Press.

Chapter 10

The Art and Artistry of
Nina Crews:
Picture Books as Springboards
for Dictation in Preschool

D A N I E L R. M E I E R

That's how it will be. I think I'll go soon. And then I'll catch the moon.
—Nina Crews, *I'll Catch the Moon* (1996)

NINA CREWS IS the author of award-winning children's books that combine adventurous stories and innovative photographs. Her settings are often urban landscapes and her child characters are often from multiracial backgrounds and varied cultures. Her books include *One Hot Summer Day* (1995), *I'll Catch the Moon* (1996), *Snowball* (1997), *You Are Here* (1998), *A High, Low, Near, Far, Loud, Quiet Story* (1999), *A Ghost Story* (2000), *The Neighborhood Mother Goose* (2004), and *Below* (2006). Her website can be accessed at http://www.ninacrews.com/books.html.

CHILDHOOD INFLUENCES

Crews was born in Germany to Donald Crews and Ann Jonas, both well-known and award-winning children's book authors and graphic designers. Crews grew up in New York City, and worked in animation before turning to picture books. She attributes much of her creativity and artistry to her parents, as well as to opportunities for play as a child.

I was brought up by creative people. My sister and I did not have structured playtime. We played together a lot and our best friends lived close by. We invented most of our games by com-

123

bining favorite toys with whatever else we might find at hand for our fantasy. We also spent a lot of time making projects. This was often a family activity. These projects were a part of our play. We made dollhouse furniture, doll clothes, and houses for our toys. My parents were ready with paints and glue and willing to help us with our ideas. We would also spend time in their studio and were allowed to use some of their professional art materials.

The kind of unstructured playtime that I experienced in my childhood encourages children to use their imagination. For example, in *You Are Here* (1998), there is a moment when the two characters Joy and Mariah use everything in the room to make a fantasy game. They fly in an airplane past a waterfall, travel to an island full of treasures, and meet a monster—and they create this trip from what is around them. My sister and I were encouraged to do this as children, to create from what was around us.

Growing up with two children's book authors and graphic designers as parents, Crews experienced her parents' books in the making, and saw first-hand how books are created and produced. From her father's work, Crews endeavored "to retain his clear and concise way of writing, and not to say more than what is needed or to over-elaborate." From her mother's work, Crews was inspired by how Ann Jonas used "things to become something else," and in her work used everyday materials to symbolize and represent something new and different.

Family and community, and especially life in the city, feature prominently in Crews's books. Her books also often contrast quiet, playful situations in children's homes with vibrant, active experiences out on the street or in the park.

I grew up in Manhattan's West Village, and enjoyed being a city kid. My first book, *One Hot Summer Day* (1995), was in response to conversations with friends who felt that the city was an unnatural place to raise children. I wanted to positively reflect a city childhood. I photographed places and textures recognizable to city children. For non-city children, I hope that my books are a fun way to experience a place that they don't know. Of course, there are many things in my photographs that will be familiar to most children no matter where they live.

Crews's books also depict and celebrate a diversity of children—varied in gender, race, ethnicity, interest, experience, family—engaged in city scenes in appealing ways.

> In *The Neighborhood Mother Goose* (2004), I wanted to present the
> characters and rhymes in a new environment that differed from
> traditional depictions. I looked at some early Mother Goose col-
> lections as I worked on the book. It was a challenge to find nurs-
> ery rhymes that would translate well to a contemporary urban
> setting. Some rhymes were better suited to this than others. I
> included well-known rhymes, some personal favorites, and some
> that I hadn't heard before researching this project. I also wanted
> to create a sense of community where the characters and places
> are all connected to one another. All of the children appear in
> more than one rhyme. The reader gets to know their faces as well
> as the neighborhood that they live in.

In her modern version of the Mother Goose rhymes, Crews depicts a diversity of children at play and socializing in the city. For "Pat-a-cake/pat-
a-cake/Baker's man," two girls clap hands on the sidewalk in front of a
bakery window. For "There was a little girl/Who had a little curl/Right in
the middle of her forehead . . . But when she was bad/She was horrid/,"
a girl is depicted about to cut the hair of a small doll. For "A was an apple
pie/B bit it/C cut it/D dealt it/ . . . X, Y, Z, and ampersand all wished for
a piece in hand/," a double-page collection of 26 children interact with
their pies on an expansive set of steps.

Such a tapestry of images—of children, adults, families, communities,
experiences—is a cornerstone of Crews's stories and books. This passion
for rendering children's lives and hopes and feelings comes from Crews's
own family and ethnic identity, from her childhood interest in play and
exploration, and her belief in honoring and celebrating children's imaginations and evolving identities.

> It is natural for me to choose to represent children of color
> in my books; as a woman of color my first impulse is to rep-
> resent children of color. Young children, though, don't really
> care about diversity first and foremost. For most young read-
> ers, one child's brown skin and another's blond hair are facts,
> not political statements. The strong message of my books and
> stories is about experiencing play and the value of imaginative
> play. Diversity is a given—a natural state of being in my stories.
> Children are reading about what will happen . . . will Jack (in
> *Below*, 2006) get Guy out of the hole? That's what's important
> to them. I do, however, think it's healthy for all children to see
> themselves reflected at some point in a story even if it's not their
> primary concern.

WELL-TOLD STORIES AND CHILDREN'S PICTURE BOOKS

For Crews, a "well-told" story takes children on a journey, an adventure, where children experience new feelings, thoughts, and perspectives.

> Children like to find a resolution to stories. If they are not satisfied with the author's resolution, they will often come up with their own version. Stories often take a reader on a journey. Sometimes this journey is a conflict that requires resolution and the journey becomes an emotional one. In my books, this conflict might simply be a bad mood or hot weather. For instance, in *One Hot Summer Day* (1995), a young girl's mother tells her daughter to play inside since it is too hot outside. But the girl wants to play outside and tries to find fun in the city heat. Later in the story, there is a rainstorm, which resolves the tension felt in the early part of the story that was caused by the oppressive heat. Her emotions are lifted through a dramatic change in the weather. She dances in the rain.

Crews's picture books often feature child characters who experience these everyday, important emotions, thoughts, hopes, and experiences of modern childhood.

> Jack (*Below*, 2006) is a character who resonates with children. It's something that children do, lose things, and they can relate to the emotion and anxiety of losing something that's important. The resolution of being able to find that important thing, as Jack does, also appeals to them. That positive resolution often does not happen in life, particularly when you are a young child—lost toys often stay lost. So this story is appealing, because the child is able to do it all.

Crews also believes that well-told stories have an underlying structure and sense of orderliness that pull children into the story world.

> There are patterns in well-told stories, patterns that are familiar and recognizable. Children appreciate this structure. In Mo Willems's books, for instance, an arc appears in his stories, where a child has certain wants and needs and then a big tantrum happens and the child cries. At the end of his stories there is always a resolution—a response to the child's initial frustration. I believe that children enjoy anticipating that positive outcome.

For Crews, the journey in artful picture books and well-told stories is also one of safety and reassurance, where children get to "return home" at story's end. In *I'll Catch the Moon* (1996), "the story is both a literal journey and also an imaginative journey." The story opens with a luminescent cityscape as seen from a child's bedroom window and with a single line of text, "Outside my window I see the city and the sky." The girl then experiences the city and the sky at night—she "holds" the moon, builds a "ladder to outer space," and climbs as "the stars will watch me, and a comet will guide my way."

> In *I'll Catch the Moon* (1996), the voice is more dreamy than my other books, and it encourages children to go off on their musings and "what if's?" whether large or small about what they know about outer space and how it works.

The story, both pictures and text, has a poetic feel and a dreamy yet active sense of movement and ease for the character. The story closes on a soft, comforting note and yet also hints at further exploration and adventure.

Part of the appeal for children of this kind of child-on-a-journey story involves the power and control given over to the story characters.

> It is important for children to have a sense of autonomy and stories of independent journeys are particularly valuable. A perfect example of this is *Stuart Little* (White, 1945). Stuart is an extremely independent little mouse who journeys off into the world. And in both *Little Bear* (Minarik, 1957) and *The Snowy Day* (Keats, 1962), an individual child experiences, explores, and solves problems on their own. The child who reads or listens to books, and who is attached to books is on a journey of the mind. That child identifies with characters that travel out into the world.

Many of Crews's books tell the story of a single character, or at most two characters, who take an "independent journey." *I'll Catch the Moon* has one character, the girl who takes her nighttime trip. *One Hot Summer Day* also has one character, the young girl who plays in the water outside. *Below* has one main character, Jack, and a supporting character, Guy, a small play figurine.

CREATING ARTFUL STORIES AND BOOKS

Crews's books are a compelling mix of text and visuals. Her text is often spare and to the point, leaving enough narrative room for readers and listeners to fill in their own text. Her photographs are carefully crafted, and work almost like photographs in a museum or art exhibit—to be studied and looked at over time, to notice small telling details and to absorb the overall feeling or idea.

> When I write a book, I think about the story and the pictures at the same time. Before I photograph, I make sketches, notes about the characters, and pull inspiration from other sources. Once the text is in good shape, I make a dummy mockup of it. I then edit the text further before I take the photographs. Once the photographs are completed, both image and text are edited together. So the two are never really far apart and always in play together.

In *You Are Here* (1998), two double-page photographs set up the story before the first page of text appears. "It was a wet and rainy day. Mariah and Joy had finished playing. They were bored . . ." begins the first page of text, as sisters Mariah and Joy are pictured with a slight scowl. As text and pictures move the story forward, the reader/listener is pulled into the playful, moment-by-moment possibilities of the two sisters' game in their living room.

> This idea of "what if?" is at work in *You Are Here* (1998), which encourages children to think of imaginative ways to play and have adventure, a good exercise for children.

This "what if?" is the pull for children, as text and picture tell us the details of each new twist in the girls' unfolding adventure.

This intertwining of text and picture, in well-told stories and books like Crews's, promotes sophisticated storytelling and story listening for young children. It asks children to follow and retain multiple storylines— of character, of plot, of language, of movement, of resolution.

> For young children learning to read, the pictures and texts are both crucial to understanding a story. Early readers are encouraged to read the images as well as the text. My books work like any good picture book—they have appealing pictures that get children to look long and hard. I try to make sure to have photos and text that help each other. Pictures can add something that

words can't show. Some pages in my books are richer than others simply because some moments in a story are more dramatic than others. Sometimes a page or spread may simply provide a transition between two dramatic moments. In other books, like *The Neighborhood Mother Goose* (2004), each spread illustrates one or more complete rhymes and there are no transition pages. This allows for pictures that are very rich in detail.

In Crews's *The Neighborhood Mother Goose*, as in other inventive children's books, the richness and variety of text and picture let children's eyes and ears linger on each page. They invite children in and hold their attention, encouraging a kind of dance in that invisible space between children as readers/listeners, the text, and the pictures.

THE BOOKS OF NINA CREWS—SPRINGBOARDS TO DICTATION

I use Crews's picture books as wonderful examples of "well-told" stories for teachers in professional development and university settings, and also in my teaching of preschool-age children as springboards to effective and high-quality dictation activities and literacy engagement. Crews's books—with spare, concise text and eye-catching and thought-provoking content and visuals—readily appeal to young children and are excellent resources for promoting children's dictation and literacy learning.

Read-Aloud Strategies

In using Crews's books and other picture books as read-alouds and for story dictation, I use several key strategies and techniques:

Careful Book Selection. I gather a small of pile of books that are related by author, content, or genre, and that I know will all work as spring boards for children's dictation. The books don't all have to be fiction, since all children benefit from a mix of fiction and nonfiction; they do, though, need to have excellent visuals, and as in Crews's books, to have a sophisticated intertwining of text and picture.

Physical Arrangement for Reading. I gather with the children on a rug area, making sure that all children can see me, the books, and one another. I always sit or kneel on the rug so I am not sitting too high; sitting close to the children adds a sense of homelike intimacy to the scene. The read-aloud can be done whole-group or small-group. But it is crucial that this book reading and sharing not always occur in a whole-group setting. Too many children can lose focus during whole-group reading and there are fewer chances for participation in a large group. It is also helpful not to have the children sitting in rows where they can't see one another. As we want children to "read the images" in books, we also want them to "read" the ideas and thoughts and feelings of their peers.

A "Hook." In a playful way, I pretend to wonder out loud about how the pile of books got by my side. "Where'd these books come? Did you bring them here? Okay, let's see what we have . . . ." Anything like this that invites children into a playful relationship and stance with children's books is important; as Crews notes, we need to connect children to the playful depiction of character in children's books and to the playful aspects of children's longing for discovery, adventure, and taking a journey.

Moving into the Story World. "There are words in this book! There are pictures in this book! How come no one told me about these? Let's see if I shake the book whether the letters and words and pictures will fall out . . ." I spin out the pretense, the magic and mystery of a children's book, as we ease into the world of a new story book. I want to pull the children along with me, to leave for the moment the here-and-now of their classroom or other setting and enter Jack's world (*Below*, 2006) on the stairs and gather around and watch (and maybe try to help) him as he tries to rescue Guy, his beloved toy figure friend, from a hole in the stairs.

Set the Story Scene. The first time I read a book, I play with the book's cover and the first inside page or two. The first two pages, even before the text appears, in *You Are Here* (1998) work so well for this. For the double-page picture just inside the cover, I say, "Whose room is this? There's a checkerboard, but I don't see anyone playing it. And there are a lot of things on the mantel piece above the fire place. Let's look and see what they are . . ." I take my cue from Crews's inviting and slightly mysterious picture, and pull the children in, asking them to pay attention with eye and ear to both the big "picture" ("Where is everybody?") in the scene and also the small "pictures" ("Is this a mask on the mantel?"). And along the way, I emphasize Crews's varied and rich vocabulary of "mantel piece" and "fireplace" and "checkerboard."

Playful and Inventive Reading. If I read a book that I have read before with the children, I maintain the playful nature of the book reading but elevate it. I sometimes start reading in the middle of the book, and read backward or forward, moving our reading around. In this playing with text and pictures, children are asked to do a slightly different kind of narrative dance—they must retain their "old" version of the story as we originally read from beginning to end while comparing it to the unfolding "new" story reading sequence.

Making It Concrete. As I read, I ask the children to use hand movements to help us physically tell the story. (This also links back to the use of hand gestures in oral storytelling, as discussed in Nadia Jaboneta's Chapter 4.) For the first page of *Below* (2006), "Jack lived in a tall, narrow house. A tall, narrow house with many stairs," I ask the children to push their arms straight up into the air to represent "tall," and we then move our arms in to represent "narrow." Most English-speaking young children, and some new language learners of English, know the word *tall,* but *narrow* is often an unfamiliar word to all young children and so the hand gestures help build a memory for the meaning of the word.

Pause and Stop. I also pause at key points in the text so that children learn to anticipate text patterns and words. In *Below* (2006), I pause at the end of the third sentence, "Jack lived in a tall, narrow house. A tall, narrow house with many stairs. Jack climbed up and Jack climbed . . . ." and I wait and let the children fill in the word *down* to complete the sentence, which in turn helps them visualize Jack's movement.

Point to the Visuals. I also point out key elements in the pictures; I want to promote children's sensitivity to the big "picture" in the unfolding story, as well as the smaller "pictures" as told in the visual details. On the third page of *Below,* Jack is shown playing with Guy on the steps with the backdrop of snowy mountains ("Jack and Guy climbed huge mountains."). On the fourth page, there is a backdrop of a city scene with a building made of wooden blocks, a traffic signal, and small cars and trucks. Children delight in pointing out the objects on these pages, and we briefly talk about the polar bear in the snowy scene and the colors of the traffic light.

Dictation Strategies

I then use several techniques to transition from the read-aloud to the next phase of story dictation in small groups:

Simple Dictation Materials. After the read-aloud, I then immediately work with a small group of children on drawing and dictation related to one of our story books. I like to have copies (preferably multiple copies) of the books right there on the table or rug with the children so they can see and re-read key sections of the books to get ideas and models for their drawing and dictation. I use blank paper, usually part of the children's dictation journal, and also markers, crayons, color pencils, and plain lead pencils.

Link Drawing and Dictation. I usually ask the children, "What do you want to draw and dictate about the story?" The children can draw and dictate some direct aspect of the story, or they can draw and dictate some aspect of their lives that relates (however tangentially) to the story. If I am met with a blank stare—they have no idea what to draw or dictate—I try several prompting strategies. I open the book and flip through the pages, hoping to engage the child in some aspect of the text and/or pictures to spark their drawing and dictation interest. Sometimes, I flip through the pages without reading or saying anything, waiting and watching the child's eyes and facial expression to see if anything catches their interest. If nothing does, I usually then re-read a bit of the text or summarize it briefly. I might also turn to the other children and ask them what they are going to draw and dictate based on the story. Or I ask a child to ask another child on their own what they are going to do. Or I give them an either-or choice: "Do you want to draw and dictate about how Jack used his crane to get Guy out *or* do you want to do the part where the dragons are in the hole?" Finally, I sometimes show the children drawings and dictation that were already completed by other children.

Talking Before Dictation. Sometimes, as the children draw, I ask them to tell me about what they are drawing. If they are preschoolers, their drawings are often not very representational, and so I do not push them in this direction. Rather, I simply show interest and get them thinking about what they are drawing and will dictate. Occasionally, depending on the child, I suggest that the children do their dictation with me first and then draw later, if they want to. Also occasionally, I ask a child to do their dictation *as* they draw—sometimes this simultaneity enriches both dictated text and drawn picture.

Honoring Children's Languages. In their dictation, I use as much of the children's verbatim language as I feel makes sense in terms of developmental appropriateness and culturally responsive teaching. I also interject as little as possible to redirect the content and direction of their dictation. If children are stuck, I use some of the strategies mentioned above. For some new language learners, who may speak little English, I often

Figure 10.1. Jack and Guy from Nina Crews's *Below*

Up came a toy soldier.
Up came a brass button
and a ball of foil lost by the cat.
Up came two pennies and a dime.
Up came Guy!

suggest particular words, phrases, or even whole sentences. Sometimes I say most of a sentence, and then pause, waiting for the child to fill in the last word. If I say a whole sentence as a possibility, the children then only have to nod or shake their head if they do or don't want the sentence. I also sometimes say a sentence or two, and then ask the children if they want to repeat the sentences back to me.

Some Dictation Examples Based on Crews's *Below*

I now provide several examples of story dictation that highlight key features of linking Crews's *Below* (2006)(see Figure 10.1) with aspects of children's early literacy learning. All of the dictation examples in this section are from preschool-age children. Example 1 comes from Jeff Daitsman's (the author of Chapter 9) teaching, and the remaining examples are from my work with preschoolers.

Example 1—Spontaneous Story Dictation. In late January, Jeff read *Below* (2006) with his preschoolers. The children loved it. As they neared the end of the story, after Guy was rescued, some of the children asked to re-read the book before they had finished the story. When they started to re-read the story, on the first page of the book, one child noticed that Jack's name started with the letter "J" just like "Jeff." Jeremy took great interest in this, as his name also started with the letter "J." Gabriella then noticed that *Guy* started with "G." Jeff and the children then proceeded to find the first letter of the names of all the children in the room on the first page of the book before continuing with the story.

When they reached the point in the story where Jack successfully rescued Guy, Gabriella came up to give Guy a kiss. Several other children did so as well, but when Jeremy did it he brushed his finger over Guy, explaining that he was knocking Guy back into the hole. Jeff told them that this meant Jack would have to rescue him again, and so Jeff turned back two pages so that Jack could do the rescue all over again. Jeff and the children did this several times until a few children began to tire of it, so Jeff finished the book, and Steven immediately wanted to tell Jeff a story (see Figure 10.2).

Steven's story combines several aspects of dictation and literacy learning. He relates it to the book that they just completed reading, which demonstrates his interest in literature and reading. He also watched Jeff's writing as he dictated and attempted to copy it on his own initiative, making a successful "R" below his dictated "R2D2." After he completed the story, Steven made a revision, clarifying that Guy fell into a hole, and thereby explaining Jack's need to look for him.

Example 2—The Tale is in the Picture. Four-year-old Dante was taken with Crews's pictures of the crane that Jack used to pull Guy out of the hole. When I read the book with the class, I had paid special attention to having the children use two hands to turn an imaginary crane and pull Guy up out of the hole. I had also used the word *crane* several times in addition to its mention in the book. Dante spent several minutes carefully using a single black marker to make swirling movements and lots of small dots. I sensed from his intensity and his focus that the drawing was the main attraction for him. And so I decided not to nudge him very far in his dictation. To start him off, I asked Dante how Jack used the crane, and then he dictated a first sentence.

Jack used the crane to get Guy out.

I then asked, "And then what happened?" In the spirit of Crews's books, with succinct and to-the-point text, Dante summed up the story's resolution:

He was happy.

Figure 10.2. Steven's Dictated Story

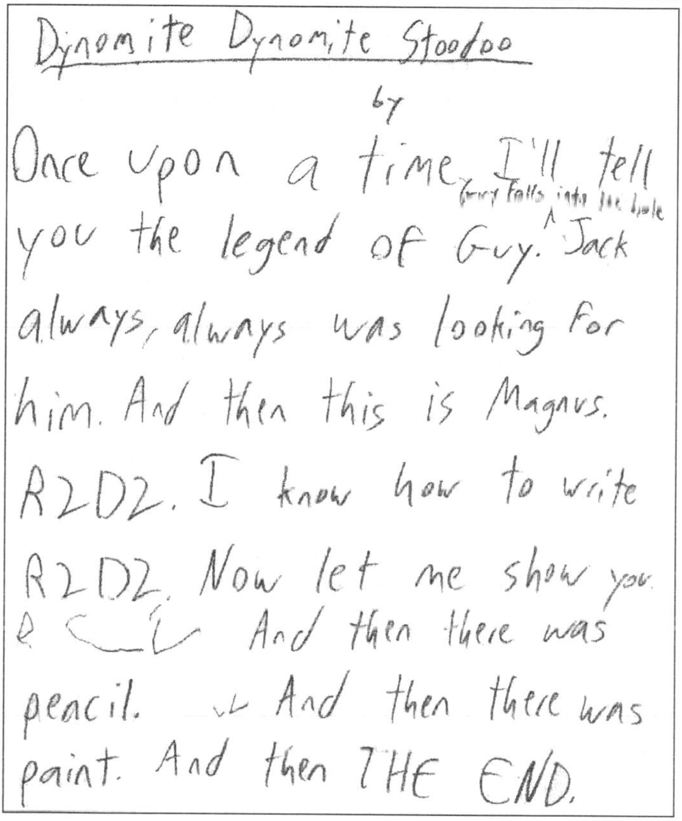

Dynomite Dynomite Stoodoo

by

Once upon a time, I'll tell you the legend of Guy. (Guy falls into the hole) Jack always, always was looking for him. And then this is Magnus. R2D2. I know how to write R2D2. Now let me show you. And then there was peacil. And then there was paint. And then THE END.

At first, I was a bit disappointed with such a spare dictated text, but then realized that for him at that moment, the main attraction was in the beautiful labor of his drawing.

Example 3—Starting Where Children Are. Not all children immediately draw and dictate content related to a children's story book. Four-year-old Sara drew three large swirly cloudlike figures in black marker, with some underlying purple in colored pencil under one black figure. She also added a humanlike head in purple in the corner. When I asked Sara what she wanted to dictate about *Below*, she started off on a tangent:

I like panda bears.

At first I hesitated, wondering if I should put this down or redirect her toward the book in a more literal and realistic way. I decided against it at least for her first sentence, and wrote it down as she said it. Sara then paused, and so I guided her back to the book. "What happened with Jack and Guy?" I asked, which prompted another sentence from Sara:

I was happy when Guy came out of the hole.

I then asked, "How did Jack get him out?" Sarah then dictated as follows:

Jack used the crane. I was happy, too. I was happy with the crane.

Sara used "I was happy" three times, but managed to place this phrase in three differently constructed sentences. Her example shows the value of starting where children are developmentally within the dictation task, and gently guiding children toward what might interest them about a story.

Example 4—Where's the Action? Four-year-old Antoine drew a swatch with a colored pencil and then drew several letterlike objects (see Figure 10.3). His dictation was based on action elements in the story:

This is the red light and the green light. It's the stoplight. It's on the stairs. Guy fell into the hole. He went down the slide. He went on the swings. What was under the hole?

With "This is the red light and the green light," Antoine links the book to his representational drawing and then to his dictation with me. The traffic light is not mentioned by Crews in the text, but I point it out in the pictures, as children love talking about what the traffic light colors mean ("Yellow means caution" and "If you don't stop at red, you can get arrested"). Antoine then dictates the central action of the story, "Guy fell into the hole," before adding details about the slide and swings, which are also not mentioned directly by Crews in the text, but are in the pictures. Antoine's closing question, "What was under the hole?", mirrors the book's closing line, "But sometimes they wondered what might be happening below." The drawing and the dictation allow Antoine to revisit the story, and to play with the key elements of text and picture that interest him.

Example 5—Story Retelling Through Pictures. For examples #5 and #6, I used my laptop computer to take down the children's dictation after we read and talked about *Below*. (See Jeff Daitsman's discussion of the use of a computer in story dictation in Chapter 9.) With my computer in my

Figure 10.3. Antoine's Drawing and Dictation Based on *Below*

3/12/08

This is the red light and the green light. It's the stop light. It's on the stairs.
Guy fell into the hole. He went down the slide. He went on the swings.
What was under the hole?

lap and a copy of *Below* in his hands, I sat next to Amar as he enthusiastically and with great fluency and speed dictated his story:

> Once upon a time there was a boy named Jack and he was working across the street. Then his friend fell down in the stairs and then he came back and they lived happily ever after. Then he put Guy right by the stairs and then he fell down. Then he was standing at the stairs waiting for Guy to come back up. He said, "Don't go under there, there are dragons. Don't go under there, there are horses. Don't go under there, there are swings. Don't go under there, there is a slide." And then Guy was coming back up. Then he asked his dad to help him get his toy back. His dad said, "I'm too busy working on the door." "No, I have to feed the baby," said his mom. Then he got his superheroes and his fire truck and then

put some police tape [the yellow caution tape] around. Then he
put the crane down and pulled Guy up. Then they were friends
forever and he never went under the hole again. The End

Amar's dictation indicates several key elements of successful literacy development:

- Excitement and enthusiasm (he is clearly delighted with the 1:1
  attention and the computer)
- Storytelling language ("Once upon a time . . .")
- Plot, scene, characters, dialogue ("His dad said, 'No, I'm too busy
  working on the door.'")
- Fluent and lively storytelling (he kept me engaged)
- Observation of the words appearing on my laptop screen as he
  dictated (oral to written language connections)
- Integration of original and new sentence structures ("Then he got
  his superheroes and his fire truck and then put some police tape
  [the yellow caution tape] around.")
- New vocabulary ("police tape" and "superheroes")
- Story extension ("Then they were friends forever and he never
  went under the hole again.")

As Amar continues his story dictation experiences with high-quality picture books like *Below* and others, the connections and transfer between
these literacy elements will only deepen and become stronger.

Example 6—Peer Collaboration and Improvisation. Jordanae and Alaya wanted to tell a story based on *Below* together. When I sat down with
both girls, I assumed that they wanted to tell their version of the story by
looking at the pictures. But with Jordanae taking the lead, I suddenly realized that they wanted to "read" the book and to become Jack and Guy.
(This is similar to Kevin wanting to *be* the truck as described in Nathan
Weber's Chapter 6). Looking at the text, and speaking in a grown-up
"reading" voice, they "read" the following text:

> Jack and Guy. We had to do it altogether. Everything that we sup-
> posed to do. The fire truck was there and they sat down together
> everyday at the green light. "One day it's going to be your birth-
> day," said Jack to Guy. Guy fell down the hole and Jack looked
> into the hole. He looked down there and all of a sudden he didn't
> have any shoes on. He saw a dragon and he became a knight.
> Then he became a cowboy. He said, "Hee haw!" He was at the

park and he slides on the slide. He was sad because he didn't know what to do. Jack told his mommy, "I lost my toy." A police man was standing by and one crane got the little boy, Guy. "Here he comes. He is back." And they sat on the stairs together. The End

Like Amar's story dictation, Jordanae and Alaya's story contains many of the same elements of successful literacy learning. They also added a few new features:

- Role-play the act of reading
- Peer-to-peer collaboration in story dictation
- Peer-to-peer negotiation during reading
- Pretense and play as they "read" the story
- Multiple roles as "readers" (looking at the text), as narrators ("The fire truck was there . . ."), and as Jack and Guy themselves ("We had to do it altogether.")

Since Jordanae and Anya dictated just after I worked with Amar, I was struck again by young children's interest in and the value of multiple pathways toward story dictation, and the need to support and extend children's individual and collaborative story dictation strategies.

THE BOOKS AND STORIES OF NINA CREWS—TAKING A PLAYFUL STANCE TOWARD STORY DICTATION

Observing the world has great value. In photography you look for things to find and that's also what a writer does. It is important to encourage children to see what they have at hand.

—Nina Crews

The books and stories of Nina Crews invite children into a world of play, imagination, action, and adventure. They celebrate the diversity of children's lives in modern childhood, and allow children from different backgrounds to relate to story book characters who go on solo journeys, confront problems and common childhood experiences, and arrive at a comforting resolution by story's end. Crews's childhood, growing up in a family of artists and storytellers with ample opportunities for imaginative play, reminds us of the origins of creativity in childhood play and storymaking.

Crews's books entice children to jump into and swim in an artistic and aesthetically pleasing world of children's picture books. With their succinct language and innovative pictures, her story books are also a powerful springboard into dictation and other language/literacy activities, where with expert adult guidance, children play with a creative and imaginative mix of words, images, and action. These kinds of language and story-rich experiences make for excellent language and literacy engagement and learning. In Crews's words, when you "look for things to find," children experience the world as photographers and writers, learning to see "what they have at hand" in their minds, their hearts, and their imaginations.

REFERENCES

Crews, N. (1995). *One hot summer day*. New York: Greenwillow Books.

Crews, N. (1996). *I'll catch the moon*. New York: Greenwillow Books.

Crews, N. (1997). *Snowball*. New York: Greenwillow Books.

Crews, N. (1998). *You are here*. New York: Greenwillow Books.

Crews, N. (1999). *A high, low, near, far, loud, quiet story*. New York: Greenwillow Books.

Crews, N. (2000). *A ghost story*. New York: Greenwillow Books.

Crews, N. (2004). *The neighborhood mother goose*. New York: Greenwillow Books.

Crews, N. (2006). *Below*. New York: Henry Holt & Co.

Keats, E. J. (1962). *The snowy day*. New York: Viking.

Minarik, E. (1957). *Little bear*. New York: HarperCollins.

White, E. B. (1945). *Stuart little*. New York: HarperTrophy.

Chapter 11

Magic and Imagination in Children's Picture Books: An Interview with Elisa Kleven

AS TOLD TO DANIEL R. MEIER

Elisa Kleven is an award-winning children's book author and illustrator. She is the author and/or illustrator of Abuela *(Dutton, 1991),* The Lion and the Little Red Bird *(Dutton, 1994), and* Our Big Home *(Millbrook, 2000) and other books for young children.* Abuela *is an ALA Notable Book, Parent's Choice Award for Illustration, and Reading Rainbow Book. Her books focus on families and the cultural life of children, and are rich in multicultural and multilingual content and illustration. More information on Elisa Kleven and her books can be found on her website at http://www.elisakleven.com/books.html.*

In this interview, Elisa Kleven gives us a behind-the-scenes look into the role of story in her books and the value of story for young children's language and literacy learning. She also describes childhood influences on her work as a writer and illustrator, the process of writing and illustrating her picture books, and places a special importance on the role of magic and imagination in children's picture books and stories.

What does story mean to you? How would you "define" it? What are its connections to the world of childhood?

I have a conventional idea of story with a beginning, middle, and an end. The stories that grab me the most in childhood and now are the ones in which the character has to solve a problem or has something they want that they don't have. My favorite book in childhood was *Charlotte's Web* (White, 1952) and this book has the ultimate problem—this little pig is facing mortality and what keeps him from dying keeps us turning the page and keeps us interested in his dilemma and predicament. Children are full of wishes, and they are powerless little people, and every day they are faced with things they want or they can't have or their own limitations, and so it is important for characters in books to reflect children's own sense of longing and wishing and their knowledge of their own problems. So a story revolves around a character overcoming an obstacle and solving a problem.

The characters I like are imperfect and have some limitation, problem, or desire. It is the job of story to solve the character's problem or grant their wish in a satisfactory way. For example, in *Sylvester and the Magic Pebble (*Steig, 1969), Sylvester finds a pebble and then he gets turned into a rock. That's quite a problem. What's going to happen to him? All of my books have characters who have problems. I usually start by making imperfect characters, something is wrong with them, something is different about them. For instance, *The Lion and the Little Red Bird* (Kleven, 1992) is a story I made about a lion whose tail the bird doesn't understand because his tail changes color. We find out that he is painting with his tail and using it as a paintbrush. It's not a life-threatening problem, it's not Wilbur facing being turned into ham and bacon, but there is something odd about this lion. I want to make the reader curious just like the little bird is curious. She has a wish—she wishes to understand the mystery about why the lion's tail changes color. At the end of the story, he rescues her from a storm and takes her into his cave and paints a picture of her. She's a little red bird. She then sees his tail changing color.

Or in *The Paper Princess* (Kleven, 1994) (see Figure 11.1), the little girl makes a lovely paper doll and it's the best thing she's ever made. She's very proud of it. Suddenly the wind whisks it away before she can give it hair. So right away that character has a problem. She's bald and she is homeless. It would be a different story if I wrote, "Once upon a time there was a girl who made a beautiful paper doll and they all had everything they wanted and sat under a tree and had a tea party. The End." There is no problem and no tension and no longing in this version. A story can have a static beginning and a happy beginning, but something has to happen. If you wrote, "Once upon a time she was the happiest little cat in the world. She had everything she needed," you would not want it to end there. You would want to say, "But then one day her owner died" or "She went out the window and got lost." Children respond to existential problems. They know that the world is a dangerous, precarious place. They have a sense of their own fragility; they are small and powerless. They like to resolve these feelings and issues through stories. It is very satisfying for children.

Figure 11.1. *The Paper Princess* by Elisa Kleven

I believe in happy endings since I am writing for young children. I don't like perfect characters or perfectly happy stories, but I do like happy endings. I don't want to give children a sugarcoated view of the world, but I owe them a satisfying and hopeful ending. Children have their own sense of limitation and powerlessness; they are full of wishes and full of longing. Through stories, children can conquer some of their fears and there is also the vicarious thrill of going off into a world that's slightly dangerous. But you are in the safety of your own room reading a story about it. For example in reading *The Paper Princess*, children see this poor little paper doll alone in the world, but knowing you are safe in your own home helps children experience the danger at a distance.

What are your childhood influences on how you envision and experience story in your books?

I was the kind of child who was full of longing, and I longed most to be in a different world from urban Los Angeles in the 1960s and 1970s. I wanted to live either in Laura Ingalls Wilder's world or the English countryside world of books like *The Secret Garden* (Burnett, 1911). I wanted to live in pioneer or romantic places or just in a purely magical world where animals talked, such as the world of *Charlotte's Web* (White, 1952). I saw the world in terms of stories. I was always making characters in my art. I cut out paper animals and made little characters out of clay and made up stories about them. My art has always been very narrative. I was not the kind of child who would sit down and draw a representational painting; I always wanted a character in my picture, and something happening to them. I didn't want just a static scene. This has carried over into my work today.

My mother was a print maker and a graphic artist. My grandmother was a sculptor. She made people and animals out of lumps of clay, which I always thought was very magical to see her transform people and animals out of clay. My mother and grandmother were both very artistic, but we all have such different styles and that is part of the beauty of it. We all work in different media and we have a different vision.

I am self-taught in my art. I have taken some drawing classes but I never went to art school. Children's books were the big influence on my work. I used to look for hours at Garth Williams's drawings because they are so beautiful and his characters have so much soul, whether they are a spider or a little girl. I loved picture books. I loved to look at Margaret Wise Brown's (1947) *The Golden Egg Book*, Ezra Jack Keats's (1962) *The Snowy Day*, and books by William Pene DuBois and Nancy Burkert. I would lose myself for hours looking at the pictures in these books.

What's the role of story in your books? How does this benefit children's language and literacy learning?

I was inspired and I internalized some of the structures of the books that I loved. From a simple book like *The Snowy Day*, where the little boy brings home a snowball and it melts in his pocket—it's a sense of loss. Or *Stuart Little*, who loses his beloved bird, there's always a sense of longing or a problem that needed solving in my favorite books. This influences me to this day.

I want to add wonder and beauty to children's lives through my stories, and also an appreciation for things that are hand-made. I never use the computer to make my books. I always use basic materials and things I cut out and paste in my collages. These materials have a very childlike feel and I have heard that this inspires children to make their own collages. They see that it is accessible, they don't have to draw perfectly, and they can make a lovely little character out of a piece of torn paper or some found object. Children also resonate with my bright colors—I want a world that is full of hope and color and warmth. I think this is important for children to have access to, especially in our over-mechanized environment. I also use language that is rich and musical, and has a beauty and a cadence and a rhythm to it. In my book *Sun Bread* (2001), the story is written all in rhyme and children respond to and absorb its rhythm. And hopefully, they will want to make their own language richer and more interesting if they are exposed to rich and interesting language in books.

How do your books celebrate children's diversity?

Diversity is part of the way that I have always seen the world. I also have interspecies pictures in my books—some pictures are filled with both crocodiles and people. I have a dreamlike, almost peaceable kingdom view of all these beings living together. Diverse children are mirrored in my books and I try to include children of all different races. I never shy away from portraying different cultures. I hope I do it in a respectful way. For instance, I am not Hispanic myself but I illustrated *Abuela* (1991, written by Arthur Dorros) and *Isla* (1995, written by Arthur Dorros) and many people have said that these books resonate with Latino children. I also love drawing different celebrations. My illustrated books *The City by the Bay* (1993, written by Tricia Brown) and *City of Angels: In and Around Los Angeles* (2008, written by Julie Jaskol and Brian Lewis) focus on different neighborhoods and communities.

What is the role of magic and pretend in your stories? What is the value of these elements for children, and also for the adults who read with and to children?

The role of magic is very prominent in my stories. I have never outgrown a deep childhood wish for magic. I wanted to fly as a child and there is a lot of flying in my stories. I wanted to talk to animals and my stories are full of talking animals. Everything is animated, which is an extension of a child's magical view of the world where everything is animate and has a soul. We unlearn this as we get older but for me it has always stayed as part of my world view. I believe that everything has a spirit or a soul. Anything can be animate. Look at characters in children's books such as *The Little Engine That Could* (Piper, 1961) or *The Stinky Cheese Man* (Scieska & Smith, 1992), these are not human or animal characters but they have a soul and a personality. That is magical. Children see the world naturally like that and children's book authors and illustrators like me re-create that sense of magic.

Magic adds fun and wonder to children's worlds. What child has not become excited about a flying character or a superhero or Peter Pan or a story of an alternate universe or different place? Suddenly, your house lands in Oz (*The Land of Oz*, Baum, 1904) or you open a door and you are in Narnia (*The Chronicles of Narnia*, Lewis, 1957) or Hogwarts (*Harry Potter*, Rowling, 1997)—children love the idea of transcending the ordinary world and being somewhere else where anything is possible.

Pretending is almost the same thing as magic. When I make a character who is a paper doll I am pretending that the doll has feelings. I am being like that little child; as an adult I am pretending. The child is inside my story, and when I make it I am also inside my story. This is similar to play. When I am deeply involved in painting a picture or making a story, I feel like I am a little child pretending. I create make-believe characters and give them stories and worlds. Children do this naturally; they are often pretending and they are naturally imaginative. The value of pretend in stories is the same as for imagination. Einstein himself said that "imagination is more important than knowledge." What would the world of stories be without imagination?

What is the relationship between dialogue and vocabulary in your stories? How do the two "live" together in the life of your stories on the page and off the page?

I do a lot with dialogue. Some of my stories are pure dialogue. My book *A Monster in the House* (1998), where a girl and a boy are discussing a monster who lives in a little girl's house (who happens to be her baby brother, we find out at the end), is done entirely in dialogue. Dialogue brings an immediacy and an authenticity to a story if you have characters saying things in their own voices to each other. I try to pepper my dialogue with interesting vocabulary. In my monster book, the boy says, "What kind of food does he eat?" And she says, "Mashed bananas with smashed up prunes and smushy peas," all the gross stuff that babies eat. And pudding jiggles on his nose and egg yolk dribbles through his toes—all fun language to make the monster come to life.

Dialogue and vocabulary both live in my stories. When dialogue comes, it just comes. I don't really plan it out. If the story calls for dialogue, I just let it flow. In *The Paper Princess* (1994), a little girl sits in the sunshine drawing a princess and I describe one page with just descriptive narrative. And suddenly the princess comes to life. She blows away and the girl says, "Wait! I didn't finish you." It goes into dialogue here. "'I'll finish myself,' the princess said in a voice as thin and new as she was." The story tells you when to use dialogue. It would have been a much flatter story if I had said, "When the princess blew away, the little girl was very sad." I want the girl to say, "Wait! Come back. I didn't finish you. You're the best thing I ever made, don't blow away." This is more effective than if I had written, "The little girl was sad because her doll blew away." She's speaking her feelings instead and this makes the story come to life.

In terms of telling a good story, how do you integrate the text and the illustrations? What is the power of this integration?

Picture books are all about the balance of text and illustration. Often the text is rather spare and the picture helps add a whole other level of meaning to the text. I often have spare text because I want children to make their own little stories, telling their own story as they look at the pictures. This lets children participate and even create a story as they look at the pictures. I want my stories to be evocative, and pictures help tell a good story. They add another level of meaning through a visual intricacy that helps tell the story.

In *Where the Wild Things Are* (Sendak, 1963), Sendak's pictures help complete his text. So when Max is chasing the dog around, Sendak does not write, "He is chasing his dog." He writes instead, "He made mischief of one kind or another." You can look at the picture and you see what kind of mischief he is making—he is chasing his pet around. A good picture book has the text and the picture working together to tell the story. In *Abuela*, the text is just, "Abuela takes me on the bus. We go all around the city." And what kind of abuela is it? She's a fun-loving grandma with stars and rainbow stripes and a sweet face and yellow stockings. She is a fun-loving, creative kind of grandmother that you can go on this imaginary flying trip with.

In terms of how I integrate text and picture, I first make a rough draft of the story. I make a text and then once it's accepted by the editor I go on to make the mock-up or dummy book where I sketch out the story and figure out where the text and pictures go. It's tricky at this point. If you look closely at some of my books, some of the text is right in the pictures, and so I leave areas in the dummy for the text to show up. And some of the text is separated from the pictures, especially when I have little contained pictures. It is really fun. I play with the design, though it needs to be planned out before I commit to the final pictures. For instance, I don't want to make a little border picture and then realize I should put text in there and there's no room. Sometimes I play around with type—as in *Sun Bread,* where the type echoes in its curve the roundness of the sun. There are a lot of design elements going into the type. I show all this in my own handwriting on my dummy.

And as for the power of this integration of text and illustration for children's language, it is very important to be visually sensitive. It helps children read the world visually as well as verbally. Sensitivity to images is very important. They are growing up in a world where advertising is always coming at them, and they have to interpret things like, "What is that ad telling me to do or be and how am I being manipulated?" It helps children think creatively, to know that there are different levels of meaning in the world. And I revise the text and pictures almost up to the time my books are printed—I fiddle a lot with my work.

Who are some of your favorite characters in your books, and how might their sense of voice, action, and individuality bring children into the world of stories?

Ernst (*Ernst,* 2002; *The Puddle Pail,* 2007) is a character who appears a lot. He's a little blue crocodile. He is a very dreamy character who has a big brother who is very down-to-earth. A lot of my characters are dreamy and artistic and kind of sensitive. They say "write what you know," and that's the kind of character I was and so that comes through in a lot of my books. I think it is important to have male characters with those qualities; a lot of little boy books are about classic, athletic, dynamic little boys and I do the dreamy, artistic boys and girls in my books.

But I like a dynamic where it is balanced out. For instance, in *Hurray, a Piñata!* (1996), Clara is the little dreamer and the very sensitive one, but we also need those good pragmatic characters who can help you solve problems and be empathic. One is not right or wrong; I just like to explore that dynamic. *The Puddle Pail* is also about the dynamic of a character whose head is in the clouds and a character who has his feet planted solidly on the ground. I like characters that reflect children and different aspects of children. In any classroom, there are those dreamers and artists, and also children who grow up to become accountants and who don't necessarily want to make things with their hands. I show both sides of that.

Characters in my books evolve as I work. I don't like static characters. I like them to learn something or change somehow, or overcome an obstacle. *The Apple Doll* (2007) is about a little girl who is afraid to start school, but she has this whole inner world, which gives her strength. She makes a little doll out of an apple to keep her company on the first day of school. On the outside, she tries to be normal and not cry but inside she is torn up a lot of the time. But she changes and grows in the course of the story.

How do teachers and families and children experience and "use" your books in and out of educational settings?

I receive email from families who say that they love my books and my characters have become part of our lives. That is incredibly gratifying to me. I received a recent email from a teacher in Virginia who said they were making a play from *The Lion and the Little Red Bird* (1992). Another teacher in California had her class act out my *The Whole Green World* (2005, written by Tony Johnston), which is a rhythmic story that I illustrated. I have heard that children act out the stories and also use them as inspiration for their own projects. Many teachers have their students make their own paper figures as in *The Paper Princess*. Any time my books serve as a springboard to children's own creativity, that is very gratifying. Some of my books have directions for projects. *Sun Bread* has a bread recipe and *The Apple Doll* has directions for making your own apple person.

Do you feel that stories are losing prominence in our culture and schools? If so, how might we bring stories back into "the fold?"

I think stories are losing prominence. With testing in schools, they are being squeezed out. Teachers need more time and freedom to use real books in the classroom, not only textbooks that are geared for testing. Teachers are swimming upstream; they have all of these pressures and have to make the time and put in the energy to make the classroom rich with real stories, real books, and real art. We need to have empathy for our children and to want their lives to be richer than what the prescribed curriculum provides at this point. It takes a love of beauty and a value of imagination.

REFERENCES

Baum, L. F. (1904). *The land of Oz*. New York: Rand McNally.

Brown, M. W. (1947). *The golden egg book*. New York: Golden Press.

Brown, T. (1993). (Illustrated by Elisa Kleven). *City by the bay*. San Francisco, CA: Chronicle Books.

Burnett, F. W. (1911). *The secret garden*. New York: HarperCollins.

Dorros, A. (1991). (Illustrated by Elisa Kleven). *Abuela*. New York: Dutton.

Dorros, A. (1995). (Illustrated by Elisa Kleven). *Isla*. New York: Dutton.

Jaskol, J., & Lewis, B. (2008). *City of angels: In and around Los Angeles*. Santa Monica, CA: Angel City Press.

Johnston, T. (2005). (Illustrated by Elisa Kleven). *The whole green world*. New York: Farrar, Straus, & Giroux.

Keats, E. J. (1962). *The snowy day*. New York: Viking.

Kleven, E. (1992). *The lion and the little red bird*. New York: Dutton.

Kleven, E. (1994). *The paper princess*. New York: Dutton.

Kleven, E. (1996). *Hurray, a piñata!* New York: Dutton.

Kleven, E. (1998). *A monster in the house*. New York: Dutton.

Kleven, E. (2000). *Our big home*. New York: Millbrook.

Kleven, E. (2001). *Sun bread*. New York: Dutton.

Kleven, E. (2002). *Ernst*. Berkeley, CA: Tricycle Press.

Kleven, E. (2007). *The apple doll*. New York: Farrar, Straus, and Giroux.

Kleven, E. (2007). *The puddle pail*. Berkeley: Tricycle Press.

Lewis, C. S. (1957). *The chronicles of Narnia*. New York: Harper Trophy.

Piper, W. (1961). *The little engine that could*. New York: Platt & Munk.

Rowling, J. K. (1997). *Harry Potter*. New York: Scholastic.

Scieska, J., & and Smith, L. (1992). *The stinky cheese man and other fairly stupid tales*. New York: Viking.

Sendak, M. (1963). *Where the wild things are*. New York: Harper & Row.

Steig, W. (1969). *Sylvester and the magic pebble*. Simon & Schuster.

White, E. B. (1952). *Charlotte's web*. New York: HarperCollins.

Chapter 12

When is a Story a Story?
The Fragmentation of Story
in a First-Grade Classroom

REBECCA AKIN

Rebecca Akin is a first-grade teacher in the Oakland Unified School District. She is a veteran teacher researcher who has taught for many years in different settings. She is also a doctoral candidate in education at Stanford University, and an active member of the Teacher as Researcher Special Interest Group of the American Educational Research Association. She is also the author of an article on teacher research in Nina Lyons and Vicky LaBoskey's (2002) edited volume, Narrative Inquiry in Practice: Advancing the Knowledge of Teaching *(Teachers College Press).*

Tomas captures first-grade classmate DeAndre on video as he reads Simms Taback's (1997) fabulously illustrated version of the story *There Was an Old Lady Who Swallowed a Fly.* DeAndre practically dances as he sits tracking with his finger and "reading" through the text, reciting the story he knows by heart. Tomas, who has become a proficient videographer, zooms in to keep DeAndre in the frame as he holds the shot and counts out loud to 10 (and in the process drowns out the actual audio of DeAndre's reading). A "10 count" is probably an outdated standard now, but it's what I know and so have taught my first graders about capturing something on videotape. "When you finally find something you think is interesting, you need to stop, focus, and hold the shot for at least 10 seconds." They've heard this refrain from me so many times they repeat it verbatim. There's a tendency, both for adults and children alike, to keep the camera moving and searching. In fact, we rarely focus in for 10 whole seconds when we're looking around ourselves with just our eyes. But the audience needs stillness to attend and make sense of what is being shown. As in any story, what is presented in video documentation is partial and purposeful. So, along with content, focus, rhythm, cadence, and balance are also essential parts of the whole process.

I USE VIDEO IN my classroom as one mode of storytelling—as one of many multimodal texts to bridge the gap for my students between the very archaic technology in use in most urban public school classrooms and their 21st-century world of imagery—video games, cable television, cell phones, Internet, and DVDs. Many of my students do not have books at home, but do have a television in their bedroom. As a "text," video is, in many fundamental ways, similar to print. In video, as with the act of composition more broadly, one generates a lot of material to reduce it down and get something useable that captures some essential part of a story.

In looking at Tomas's footage, my students and I took a dizzying ride from his 7-year-old perspective through our "silent reading time" from earlier in the day, following his footsteps as he walked around the classroom and decided where to stop as he looked through the viewfinder. As a group, we decided to cut most of his footage. There were 20 seconds of jerkiness that we recognized as a close-up of the floor followed by a prolonged shot of Eduardo's nose and mouth, then followed by the top of Alejo's head and the ceiling. All this until Tomas settled in on DeAndre. Finally, there it was—the focus that Tomas found promising. Stilling himself, he adjusted the zoom to center DeAndre, and kept the lens steady while he counted, "One . . . two . . . three . . . four . . . five . . ." slowly to 10 until we see what he is focusing on.

Admittedly, I'm the one amazed by what he's captured and in my excitement clearly indicate that this is a shot we will use. Given both time constraints and issues around accessibility of our school's mobile MacLab, I'm also the one who will edit the final video piece that will tell the story of some of the learning opportunities in our classroom. The logistics of my role as editor is problematic; editing anything entails deciding what is and what is not important, and what constitutes a central piece of the telling of a story. I am troubled as I think about what I am asking my students to do. Whose story will this be? What, really, is it a story of? And the question that's been with me this whole year, what makes something a story? Although I don't think I realized it until June, these were not incidental or isolated questions. I spent the whole year exploring these questions in relation to the stories that were incorporated into our classroom life.

WHERE IS THE STORY IN A SCRIPTED READING PROGRAM?

I have 18 boys in my first-grade class of 20 students and I look for any effective strategies to keep them engaged while reading, being read to, and engaging with stories. This idea of engaging with stories, however, is fraught with contradictions in my classroom. Our district adopted a scripted phonics-based program that constitutes our entire language arts curriculum. The program is explicitly a reading program and consequently has a minor writing component. Part of the issue with the marginalization of writing is time. We devote the entire morning to our language arts curriculum—from 8:40 A.M. to our 11:35 A.M. lunch break. And we still do not have enough time to cover everything specified in the teacher's manual. Time, or the lack of it, is a huge issue.

Admittedly, I struggle with the appropriate implementation of our scripted program, which is part of the reason it takes so long to cover. This is my first year using the program, and I have found this highly scripted program ironically difficult to figure out. It is embarrassing to me that a program that is essentially "teacher-proof" has been complicated for me to implement. There are so many different components and so much to cover daily, there is a vigorous pacing guide, there are many unique aspects to the program's way of doing things, a great deal of program-specific vocabulary, and, possibly the most challenging, many elements that go against my better judgment. This is my eighth year teaching, with 7 spent in kindergarten, first grade, or a combination of both. I have a lot to learn, but I also have a good deal of experience reading and writing with 4- to 7-year-olds.

Part of what is so counterintuitive about the scriptedness of our program is the absence of room for improvisation when it comes to both the required stories and the conversations around them. There are probably teachers who can use the program brilliantly and still find time to incorporate outside literature, or take the story and book conversations in directions initiated by the children. I do not mean to vilify the program. I initially started the program with a healthy skepticism, and have learned a great deal from using it. My students can decode like demons, which has never been the result of my teaching prior to using this curriculum. But in many ways, ironically, the program has made me a better teacher because I am constantly pushing against what I am asked to do. The issues raised around how the curriculum both uses and provides opportunities for stories are at the heart of much of my pedagogical frustration.

There are, essentially, two types of story readings in our required language arts curriculum. The first almost doesn't count. It is the reading of short decodable books—often two or three each day—which students read "independently" in some way. In my class, because these books proved too challenging for my students, we read the books through choral reading, echo reading, and/or partner reading. These decodable books are not stories per se, but more like short scenes that unfold through a focus on text with a particular spelling pattern and two or three high-frequency words that the children are supposed to know. The stories are not quite nonsensical, but close. The content is not predictable, and the images do little to give clues about the text. We never refer to them as "stories" and they are appropriately seen by the students as decoding exercises. A number of my students do not expect there to be any sense-making in this process, only sounding out of words with a few recognizable sight words and noting new vocabulary words.

The second kind of story reading in the program are the read-alouds used for comprehension instruction. In general, the program draws on trade book literature. Although presented in either big book form or in one of three readers, the stories are actual published stories, not ones written by the publisher. To say we do a read-aloud, however, pushes the boundaries of what this normally means in a primary grade classroom. Stories in the curriculum are presented as "instructional opportunities." They are not ways of representing and thinking about the world that allow what Anne Haas Dyson (1993) refers to as the essential social work of understanding human relationships through sustained engagement with stories and story books.

Depending on the time of year and the particular program unit, one story generally stretches over 2 to 4 days. There is rarely a complete reading through of a story in one sitting. We might be asked to browse through a whole story, but particularly in the second half of the year, the reading is designed to happen in numerous parts. Many of my students express frustration with this strategy. If the reading of a story spans 2 days, the children are generally still eager by the second reading. But stories that are supposed to last 3 or 4 days are met with loud protests and a very clear, pronounced lack of engagement.

Much of the reasoning for this breaking apart of a story is because there is so much instructional ground to cover in the curriculum. For instance, there are specified pauses in the reading for me to pose comprehension questions. I stop often to emphasize both grammatical and spelling conventions. I stop again to articulate my own internal reading strategies. If we were to read the whole story and cover all of the instructions marked by the manual, we would be sitting for much too long. While I would never argue that instructional opportunities should be missed, I question what happens to the essential forms and functions of the story in the process. So I ask myself, "When does a story lose its essence as a story?"

There's a cadence and a rhythm that add to the meaning and beauty of reading and listening to a story, both fiction and nonfiction, that is lost when a story is chopped into segments and dissected. I find this true for all stories, but particularly stories for young children. Although I understand the value of stopping and asking questions, or pausing to make an occasional remark, prediction, or note something of importance, we never read through a story as a story for the joy or the sense of it. Stories in our program are instead used as instructional opportunities to emphasize spelling patterns, specific vocabulary, grammatical conventions, comprehension skills, and comprehension strategies. I now see more clearly, though, that stories in and of themselves are not instructional opportunities.

READING AND WRITING STORIES

It was clear to me throughout the year that the way I used stories in our language arts curriculum was very limited and limiting. However, it was not until May that I made the connection between story reading and the pronounced lack of writing in the curriculum. Toward the end of the year, I asked my students to begin writing about things they had learned during their first-grade year. I know this is a hard task developmentally for 7-year-olds, but I wanted them to think back on the year and take stock, in their first-grade way, of either something that was meaningful to them or something that happened. I provided various different scaffolds. We brainstormed. We used different concept maps. I wrote frames for sentences. I modeled the various types of writing I hoped they would produce. We wrote together. Nothing seemed to be generative or helpful in getting them started. Some students refused to write. Others wrote, but didn't produce much. Still others reproduced the list we brainstormed together. After my initial frustration, I took their reluctance, hesitancy, or inability as my failure rather than theirs.

In truth, we have done little writing this year. Our nonfiction writing in particular has come almost entirely through the science curriculum. Anything autobiographical or reflective that happened through our language arts curriculum felt minimal. Part of the challenge of the program's writing piece is that it is typically unrelated to the program's reading curriculum. Out of the blue, seemingly, I am asked to teach the genre of letter writing, and this to an imagined audience and focusing primarily on the layout of a standard letter format rather than the letter's purpose and message. In another random week, I am to teach writing informational signs. Often, but also equally arbitrarily, we find ourselves revisiting descriptive writing. Rarely does the writing relate to our reading stories or to anything we are doing in class. My students and I comply, but the work—some of it in workbooks—becomes merely an exercise, not the creation of something meaningful.

The examples of narratives provided through the program's read-alouds are presented in fragments. There is no sense of a whole and very little clear connection to our lives. A sense of fluency and story flow are not modeled anywhere. Most significantly, the concept of the "storying" of experience (Clandinin & Connelly, 2000) is completely lacking for my students as an academic expectation. They know how to tell a story—they came to me from kindergarten and through oral language experiences from home with that ability—but there has been a clear absence of academic opportunities for my students to read, write, tell, and listen to complete stories on a regular basis. Equally significant, our scripted curriculum provides no formal experience with story structure, neither through listening to stories nor in the minimal writing instruction.

Is There a Story Here?

I wanted an end-of-year "product" that would provide the vehicle for my students to collect and "story" their first-grade experiences. So I pulled out my video camera both to capture and help them reflect on the collection of learning activities we engaged in on a daily basis over the year. Although video work is something I am drawn to personally, I am not an advocate for various kinds of multimodal literacies to replace reading and writing texts in the traditional sense, particularly with young children who are just learning how to put words on paper. But at this point I was at a loss. If they weren't comfortable with writing in May, there was a limit to what I could teach them in the last month of June. Still, I wanted them to tell some kind of story about their first-grade year.

I have done a fair amount of videotaping myself, but I had never before put a video camera in the hands of a first-grade student. When it was someone's turn, I showed him or her individually how to hold the camera, how to watch through the LCD screen, how to tell if the shot is square, and how to zoom in and out. The larger task of critique fell to the whole class when we all watched the pieces that the students took that day or the day before. We then engaged in technical talk about the quality of the shot, which was mostly teacher-directed conversation. The work of documenting and viewing the video very quickly became part of classroom life like our other daily routines.

But, to my surprise, two very unexpected things then happened. First, the children took every aspect of this work completely seriously. We did some storyboarding to start, and without exception, all of my students conceptualized and took notes on what they thought should be included in the story. This level of engagement had not happened previously when we tried to write. I also made it clear that any playing to the camera would get cut out in the editing process. As a result, everyone made an extra effort to focus in on their work when the camera was pointed at them. The children took ownership of this project, unlike previously when they tried to write about their experiences.

Second, most students provided first-person narration about the video they were shooting. Although I hadn't suggested, modeled, or even thought of this, almost all students narrated some aspect of what they were doing while they were filming. Since the camera did not have an external microphone, I resigned myself to knowing this project would become essentially a video piece. However, the camera's microphone did capture the comments of the child who was videotaping. As a result, the children's thoughts about what they saw were recorded, and this audio piece became a collaborative running narrative.

For example, Mario watched DeAndre as he pointed the camera on Dante who was working with tangrams. DeAndre and Mario spoke to the camera and to one another:

> *DeAndre:* Dante working hard.
> *Mario:* Yep. Dante's working really hard.
> *DeAndre:* Hey Dante! You working hard! (Dante looks up, smiles, nods, and continues working)
> *Mario:* Why did Ernesto have to walk in front of the camera like that? (Ernesto had just walked in front of the shot) We're gonna have to cut that out.
> *DeAndre:* Yeah, Dante working really hard.
> *DeAndre:* Hey! Look! Look! I can even see the lines up in there. You know, the black lines? (He had just zoomed in on the lines of the tangram puzzle.) Yeah, Dante working hard.

Students also often gave a running account of what they were choosing to capture, as with Tomas's taping:

> *Tomas:* (holding the camera on Fernando) Now Fernando's coming up. Here's a shot of Fernando writing about oceans. One, two, three, four, five, six, seven, eight, nine, ten. (holding the camera on Kytel) Now Kytel coming up. Here's one on Kytel writing on the carpet. You're next, Ernesto.

This kind of language—social and in the moment—was typical of the children's voice-over narration. It was uncomplicated, direct, and often just a simple running commentary. They were verbalizations of thoughts that happened while students filmed and they certainly did not in themselves tell any kind of story. In an odd way, they were similar to the kind of metacognitive stepping back and analyzing that was supposed to happen

in our language arts program with the read-alouds. A significant difference in the case of the video commentary, however, was that the students were the ones deciding what was important, both in terms of decisions about what to film and the thoughts they spoke while filming. Even
though I was the sole producer, the children quickly gained an important
sense of ownership over the process of narratively constructing and ver-
balizing thoughts about our videotaped story.

As things progressed, though, I realized that one aspect of the videotaping project involved fragmentation. It is specifically the fragmentation
of stories that I had assumed was only a problem in our scripted curriculum, and that made stories seem, somehow, to lose their essence. We were
organized and purposeful in the videotaping, but given our frantic cur-
ricular pace, students could never anticipate when they would be called
on to tape. In fact, I usually remembered after an activity or lesson had
started that someone had previously decided that we needed to tape this
kind of activity. I would then find a student who had noted through our
storyboarding that this was an important activity, put the video camera
in his or her hand with little warning, and let the child tape until either
the camera became too heavy or the lesson was over. Also, because of
movement, indecipherability, and lack of focus in much of their footage,
only partial bits of what each student taped could be used. Since there
were also 20 student pieces to incorporate in the final video, only a small
selection of each student's work could actually be used in the end. Fragmentation seemed not only inevitable, but in some ways prohibitive for
the structuring of any kind of story. If nothing else, central to a well-told
"story" is some kind of thread that holds it together and provides a focus.
At the time, it wasn't clear that the overarching theme of what my first
graders learned that year was a strong enough thread to hold the piece
together.

In an attempt to make the video tell a more cohesive story, I interviewed each student about what they learned, liked, disliked, or thought
about their first-grade year. I pulled excerpts from these interviews to
intersperse throughout their individual video pieces. On their advice, I
also assembled the video in a narrative structure that was linear and sequential. It started with a sequence of the children lining up outside in
the morning. It then proceeded throughout the structure of a normal day,
with language arts activities followed by lunch, math time, and continuing on until dismissal. Even though what the viewer saw were bits and
pieces of our day, the sequence had a familiarity and a flow that, seen
altogether, made for a coherent whole.

The final video was long—23 minutes. We watched it at our year-
end Open House. Most students fell in and out of concentration. There

were side conversations, of which I am normally very intolerant. It was "their" video, however, so I restrained myself from reprimanding and finally gave up and just let them talk. But when I listened in to their side conversations, I realized that their talk was completely on task. The children commented on the pieces they were seeing—what order things were happening in, who seemed to be present the most, who was working with whom, who was videotaping, what was happening outside the frame, what happened before and after the camera was trained on a shot and there was a continuation of the talk that they had engaged in on the video. They were making comments not unlike those that they made during the perusal of nonfiction texts more generally, where they would put themselves in the story. In essence, I was pleased to see that they were telling stories related to the story shown in the video. This spontaneous and interactive conversation was yet another layer of the project's powerful form of storytelling, and one that was performative in that it added a dynamic component to the actual text (Denzin & Lincoln, 2000).

In the end, I could not tell if the actual story in the video mattered to my students. But there were several factors involved in the children's storytelling that were illuminating for me. There was a fluidity in the process of the "telling" and their documentation work together: They chose what to videotape and did the video taping themselves. There was also a sense of resonance—they seemed to find themselves in the story: They knew subject matter well, they were the characters, and what they captured was their own engagement in everyday class work. There was choice: They videotaped and, therefore, were the ones who decided what to capture. There was flexibility: After watching the footage, we revised and edited what we thought was important to capture and keep. There was a cadence, rhythm, and flow to the finished piece, created in part by the story's familiar structure and the children's own narration.

BEYOND STORY FRAGMENTATION—CLOSING THOUGHTS

In the end, as I watched my students' engagement with the story construction process in our video project, I came to a deeper understanding of what it might mean to ask "What makes a story a story?" There is no question that the stories included in our language arts curriculum were stories, but the way they were presented and received by my students made me wonder if the children were understanding these stories as mere exercises in comprehension skills and strategies rather than as complete stories. This, in turn, made me realize that I myself didn't know what it meant for something to be a story.

Having struggled with this issue all year, I now find myself at a place where I realize it is not so important to know whether something is a story. I asked the wrong question, or perhaps it is one better left for a more theoretical conversation. Rather, what is helpful in continuing to teach with any curriculum that fragments stories is having a clear understanding of what stories provide students in terms of language and literacy learning. I can easily generate a list of what I learned about story from our video project: Resonance seems central when engaging with a text, as does flexibility; cadence and rhythm add coherence; coherence in turn provides something to connect to; ownership is important, even if it simply means having the right to ask questions and go on meaningful tangents for the children; and finally, the creation of some type of relationship to the story and the world is essential for meaningful engagement. However, like my question about what makes a story a story, I imagine that this list will also at some point seem not quite the right way to think about quality engagement with stories.

Looking ahead to next year, I will still have the complication of negotiating both a scripted curriculum and the time constraints of a rigorous pacing guide. The stories throughout my language arts block will still be presented in fragments and focused around discrete instructional points. But, as I learned this year, finding time in the margins of the day for engagement with our own stories is essential for me and for the students. What feels most fruitful and possible, however, is ongoing inquiry and watching children in authentic story experiences and noting what "works," what resonates, what they find engaging, and where our questions, interests, and connections take us.

REFERENCES

Clandinin, J., & Connelly, M. (2000). *Narrative inquiry: Experience and story in qualitative research*. San Francisco: Jossey-Bass.

Denzin, N., & Lincoln, Y. (Eds.). (2000). *Handbook of qualitative research* (2nd ed.). Thousand Oaks, CA: Sage.

Dyson, A. H. (1993). *Social worlds of children learning to write in an urban primary school*. New York: Teachers College Press.

Taback, S. (1997). *There was an old lady who swallowed a fly*. New York: Viking.

Epilogue

Jack and Guy. We had to do it altogether
                    —Jordanae and Alaya (4-year-olds retelling Nina Crews *Below*)

Basically, in school it is assumed that a story, written or otherwise, is separate from you, has a beginning and an end, and is something you fix, frame, give meaning to. At home . . . the opposite was true: Story is not separate from you, has no beginning and end, and is not something you can fix or frame in any way. Rather, a story is something that lives with you forever, something that can be relevant in a multitude of ways and situations.
                    —Greg Sarris (in Krupat & Swann, 2000)

IN PUTTING this book together, I now more clearly see and feel and hear the power of story for children's successful language and literacy learning. I now feel even more strongly that story must become a critical force in our teaching for it to have a more powerful place in our children's lives. We must now strengthen our conceptual understanding of effective language and literacy teaching by seeing how story connects children's words, ideas, feelings, achievement, and sense of self. We must also strengthen our pedagogical practices by inviting story to become a more frequent and prominent guest in our classrooms. As the chapters in this book attest, there are multiple ways for both teachers and children to reclaim story as a hallmark of effective and high-quality language and literacy education and learning.

STORIES AND DEVELOPMENT

In this book, several authors remind us of the value of looking at our work with our youngest children to see where a love of and attachment to stories can begin in human development. For example, Erica Almaguer and Gena Wilson, co-authors of their chapter, remind us of the inherent rhythm and musicality of stories, and how much valuable and long-lasting language learning begins in the story experiences of infants and toddlers. Todd Wanerman shows how story drama and story reading can be intimately connected to young children's dramatic play and their sensory exploration of self, others, and the physical world. Kim Hughes, in looking at the value of social stories, discusses how new language learners gain multilingual skills through a comforting sense of social support and bonds with peers, teachers, and family members. Jeff Daitsman, working with preschoolers, shows how story dictation with "preliterate" children brings their oral words closer to the written word, and how play with words and sounds and ideas provides meaningful early literacy engagement.

Taken together, these authors remind us that we must look beyond the current policy emphasis of language and literacy standards and expectations for a particular age group or grade. Story is a universal feature of the human experience, and if we can bring story into daily language and literacy practices, we can begin linking children's experiences across so-called age and grade boundaries. In this way, the musicality of stories and rhymes for babies becomes linked to the delight of shared stories with toddlers, which in turn becomes linked to the oral/written dictated stories in preschool, and so on. This kind of conceptual and pedagogical linking, then, gives us a much-needed "developmental thread" for using and engaging with stories from birth through the elementary school years.

STORIES AND CHILDREN'S LIVES

Other contributors in this book examine how we can make stories relevant to children's lives—who they are as individuals and as members of particular communities. Patricia Sullivan, in focusing on superheroes and their stories, shows how even young children are more than capable of and interested in taking critical stances on important topics and issues in their lives and the world around them. Lori Oldham discusses how she makes room in her highly scripted language arts curriculum for personal stories in her bilingual kindergarten, and how this process breaks down barriers between home and school. Nina Crews, the children's author, explains how her stories and picture books celebrate the lives of city children, and feature solo children going on important journeys within a comforting "sense of community." Elisa Kleven, another noted children's book author, discusses how her books entice children into a literary world of magic and imagination, and encourage children's universal sense of curiosity and "wonder."

These contributors remind us that compelling and well-told stories reaffirm where children come from, who they are, and where they might go. Stories help children hold onto certain universals in childhood—magic, play, discovery, adventure, danger, safety, fears, hopes, and dreams—and to do so in ways that touch individual children's lives. Stories can both universalize and particularize the human experience, enticing individual children into new communities of learners, thinkers, readers, talkers, listeners, and tellers. In this way, stories give us a starting point—ourselves—as well as other points farther down the teaching/learning road that involve the lived experiences and narratives of others.

STORIES AND UNDERSTANDING OUR TEACHING

Still other contributors to this book look at their role as practitioners and as professionals in linking story with children's language and literacy learning. Nadia Jaboneta discusses how a professional storyteller in her classroom became an in-house form of professional development, and how she was inspired and motivated to become a storyteller herself through the professional storyteller's modeling and techniques. Nathan Weber, looking at wordless books with young new language learners, found that close inquiry on how his children engaged with the books helped him resee and reconceptualize the value of child-centered language instruction. Inas Deeb and Valerie Jakar, in their work with teachers in Israel and East Jerusalem, reflect on new ways to support and extend the work of teachers interested in promoting more powerful language and literacy teaching through story books. Finally, Rebecca Akin reflects on a year's involvement with story in her scripted first-grade curriculum, and learns anew the value of self-refection for meaningful language and literacy engagement.

These authors remind us that we can't use stories to strengthen our curriculum and teaching if we don't also examine our own goals, methods, expectations, and assumptions. All of which, of course, takes time and energy and a deep appreciation and respect for seeing all of teaching and learning as one big set of unfolding stories. In this way, it is impossible to script and guarantee the teaching and the learning of language and literacy behaviors; this story has not been told or written yet. The storying, rather, will evolve through the intermingling of children's behaviors and ideas and words and our teaching goals, strategies, reactions, and reflections. We will never quite know the full story that is coming our way in our language and literacy work with children, but we can continually tighten the connections between our roles and thinking as teachers and the children's roles and thinking as students.

As 4-YEAR-OLDS Jordanae and Alaya know ("Jack and Guy. We had to do it altogether."), children can become story readers, tellers, narrators, characters, objects, and so on more easily than we might think. Children

are the ones who know how to do everything with stories "altogether."
Children know that there is really no other way. As adults, far from our
own childhoods, we've strayed from this fact of story life, and need to be
reminded from time to time of the eternal power of stories to keep the
heart and the mind close to the beat of childhood, close to the rhythm
and sounds of our earliest words, close to the playfulness of our earliest
ideas and feelings. The authors of this book hope that we have helped you
in this process of remembering and of moving forward, and we support
and applaud your future efforts to give story a more prominent place in
children's language and literacy learning.

REFERENCE

Sarris, G. (2000). From a place called Santa Rosa. In A. Krupat & B. Swann (Eds.),
    Here first: Autobiographical essays by Native American writers (p. 304). New York:
    Modern Library.

Index

About the Editor

Daniel R. Meier is Professor of Elementary Education at San Francisco State University. His teaching and research interests are language and literacy education, narrative and teacher research, and international education. He is the author of *Learning in Small Moments—Life in an Urban Classroom* (1997); *Scribble Scrabble—Learning to Read and Write* (2000); *The Young Child's Memory for Words—Developing First and Second Language and Literacy* (2004); and, with Barbara Henderson, *Learning from Young Children in the Classroom—The Art and Science of Teacher Research* (2007). He also serves as coeditor of *Voices of Practitioners*, an online journal of the National Association for the Education of Young Children (http://www.journal.naeyc.org/btj/vp/) that promotes teacher inquiry.